Ralph Harry Vincent

The Elements of Hypnotism

The Induction of Hypnosis, its Phenomena, its Dangers and Value

Ralph Harry Vincent

The Elements of Hypnotism
The Induction of Hypnosis, its Phenomena, its Dangers and Value

ISBN/EAN: 9783337277437

Printed in Europe, USA, Canada, Australia, Japan

Cover: Foto ©Thomas Meinert / pixelio.de

More available books at **www.hansebooks.com**

THE
ELEMENTS OF HYPNOTISM

THE INDUCTION OF HYPNOSIS,
ITS PHENOMENA, ITS DANGERS AND VALUE

BY

R. HARRY VINCENT

WITH TWENTY ILLUSTRATIONS
SHOWING EXPERIMENTS

LONDON
KEGAN PAUL, TRENCH, TRÜBNER & CO., Ltd.
PATERNOSTER HOUSE CHARING CROSS ROAD
1893

PREFACE.

THIS book has been written in the endeavour to meet a want which has often been pointed out to me. Within its pages I have tried to give a simple account of the nature and effects of hypnotism—to show how the state is produced, and what it is.

It is not, perhaps, the easiest thing in the world for a writer, on such a subject, to treat his theme popularly, and, at the same time, scientifically; and I am conscious of very many faults.

The use of technical terms has been avoided, and controversial questions have not been much discussed, as this would have led me too far from my original purpose.

I think it well to say, here, that I trust this book will lead no one to rashly experiment with hypnotism; the dangers of its ignorant practice are almost innumerable and very serious; and, whilst it has partly been my object to show the value and importance of a proper use of hypnotism, it is by no means my desire to minimise the dangers of its abuse.

My sincere thanks are due to Dr C. Lloyd Tuckey, for his kindness in revising the chapter on the medical aspects of the question; to Dr W. Pickett Turner, for his assistance in the preparation of many of the illustrations accompanying the text; and to Mr Lindisay Poulter, for revising the proof sheets.

R. HARRY VINCENT.

OXFORD, *October* 1893.

CONTENTS.

	PAGE
CHAPTER I.	
THE GENESIS OF HYPNOTISM	1
CHAPTER II.	
THE LATER HISTORY OF HYPNOTISM	35
CHAPTER III.	
MENTAL ACTION	80
CHAPTER IV.	
THE INDUCTION OF HYPNOSIS	128
CHAPTER V.	
THE PHENOMENA OF HYPNOSIS	159
CHAPTER VI.	
THE DANGERS OF HYPNOTISM	221
CHAPTER VII.	
THE VALUES OF HYPNOTISM	235
CHAPTER VIII.	
THE "TRANSFER" EXPERIMENTS	252
CHAPTER IX.	
HYPNOSIS IN ANIMALS	258
APPENDIX	263

ILLUSTRATIONS.

		PAGE
I.	"Fascination"	164
II.	The Suggestion of Fighting	166
III. IV. }	The Idea of "a" Lost	182
V.	Absence of Ability to Spell	184
VI.	"Intoxication"	185
VII.	"An Heavenly Vision"	186
VIII.	"Toothache"	188
IX.	"Mirth"	190
X.	"Grief"	192
XI. XII. {	Changed Personality— Writing as a little Girl	} 196
XIII. XIV. {	Signature under Hallucination of Personality	198
XV.	Writing under Suggestion of Intoxication	198
XVI.	Frog Catalepsed	261
XVII.	Frog Catalepsed	261
XVIII.	Snake Catalepsed	261
XIX.	Toad Catalepsed	261
XX.	Lizard Catalepsed	261

AUTHORS QUOTED AND REFERRED TO.

AUGUSTINE, ST. *De Civitate Dei.*
ANDRY. *Rapport des Commissaires.* 1784.
BAILLY, P. R. *Rapport des Commissaires.* 1784.
BÉRILLON, Dr EDGAR. *Revue de l'Hypnotisme.* Oct. 1890.
BERNHEIM, Prof. H. *De la suggestion et des ses applications à la thérapeutique.* English translation. London, 2nd ed. 1890.
BINET (ET FÉRÉ). *L'animal magnétisme.* Paris. English translation. London, 3rd ed., 1891.
BOUILLARD. *Rapport des Commissaires.* 1837.
BURDIN (jeune) (ET DUBOIS). *Histoire Académique du Magnétisme animal, etc.* Paris, 1891.
BURCKHARDT. *Revue de l'Hypnotisme.* Aug. 1888.
BURGGRAV, J. G. *Cura Morborum magnetica.* 1611.
BUROT, Prof. *Revue de l'Hypnotisme.* Dec. 1888.
BRAID, Dr JAMES. *Neurypnology.* London, 1849, etc., etc.
CAILLE. *Rapport des Commissaires.* 1784.
CARPENTER, Dr. *Mental Physiology.*
CAVENTON. *Rapport des Commissaires.* 1837.
CHARCOT, Prof. J. M. *Comptes rendus de l'Académie des Sciences. Magnetism and Hypnotism. The Forum,* 1890, etc.
CLOQUET. *Rapport des Commissaires.* 1837.
—— *Details des cures opérées à Buzancy.* 1784.
CORNAC. *Rapport des Commissaires.* 1837.
COURMELLES, Dr Foveau de. *Hypnotism.* London, 1892.
D'ARCET. *Rapport des Commissaires.* 1784.
DE BORY. *Rapport des Commissaires.* 1784.
DELŒUF, Prof. J. *Revue de l'Hypnotisme.*
DELEUZE, J. P. F. *Histoire Critique du Magnétisme animal.* Paris, 1813.
DIGBY, Sir KENELM. *Of the cure of wounds by the powder of sympathy.* London, 1660.

DUBOIS (d'Amiens). *Rapport des Commissaires.* 1837.
—— (ET BURDIN, jeune). *Histoire Académique du Magnétisme animal.* Paris, 1841.
DUMONTPALLIER, Dr A. *Revue de l'Hypnotisme.* Aug. 1890.
EMERY. *Rapport des Commissaires.* 1837.
FÉRÉ, Dr C. *Les hypnotiques hystériques considerées comme sujets d'experience, etc.* Paris, 1883.
FÉRÉ (ET BINET). *L'animal Magnétisme.* Paris, 1887.
FOISSAC. *Rapports et discussions de l'Académie Royale sur le Magnétisme animal.* Paris, 1833.
FOREL, Prof. A. *Der Hypnotismus.* Stuttgart, 1890.
FOUQUIER. *Rapport de l'Académie Royale.* 1833.
FRANKLIN. *Rapport des Commissaires.* 1784.
GLOCENIUS, ROD. *Tract. de Magnet. vuln. curat.* Marburgi, 1608.
GUERSENT. *Rapport de l'Académie Royale.* 1833.
GUILLOTIN. *Rapport des Commissaires.* 1784.
GURNEY, EDMUND. *Proceedings of Society for Psychical Research.*
GURY, S.J. *Compendium Theologiae Moralis.*
HAMMOND, Dr. *Spiritualism and Nervous Derangement.*
HEHL, MAXIMILIAN, S.J. *Tabulae Solares, etc., etc.* 1763.
HEIDENHAIN, Prof. R. *Hypnotism.* London, 1892.
HEINSIUS. *Beytrage zu meinen Versuchen, etc.* Leipsig, 1776.
ITARD. *Rapport de l'Académie Royale.* 1833.
JUSSIEU, A. L. DE. *Rapport de l'un des commissaires, etc.* Paris, 1784.
KINGSBURY, Dr G. C. *The Practice of Hypnotic Suggestion.* Bristol, 1891.
KIRCHER, A., S.J. *Magnes sive de Arte Magnetica.* Coloniae, 1643, etc., etc.
KRAFFT-EBING, Prof. R. VON. *Eine experimentelle Studie auf dem Gebiete des Hypnotismus.* 2nd Ed. Stuttgart, 1890. English translation. London, 1890.
LAVOISIER. *Rapport des Commissaires.* 1784.
LEHMKUHL, A., S.J. *Theologia Moralis.*
LEROUX. *Rapport de l'Académie Royale.* 1833.
LE ROY. *Rapport des Commissaires.* 1784.
LIÉBAULT, Dr. *Du Sommeil et des États Analogues.* Paris, 1866; New Ed., 1889.
LJÉGOIS. *De la suggestion, etc.* Paris, 1888.
LUDWIG. *Dissert de Magnetismo in corpore humano.* Leipsig, 1772.

AUTHORS QUOTED AND REFERRED TO. xiii

LUYS, Dr. *Clinical Lectures on Hypnotism. The Recent Discoveries in Hypnotism. The Fortnightly Review,* June and August 1890.
MAJAULT. *Rapport des Commissaires.* 1784.
MANDUYT. do. 1784.
MARC. *Rapport de l'Académie Royale.* 1833.
MARTIAL. Book III.
MAXWELL. *De Medicina Magnetica.* Frankfort, 1679.
MESMER. *De influxu planetarum, etc.,* 1766. *Memoir sur la découverte du magnétisme animal.* Paris, 1779. *Precis historique des faits relatifs au magnétisme animal.* Paris, 1781. *General Explanations of Magnetism.* Carlsruhe, 1815, etc.
MOLL. *Der Hypnotismus.* Berlin, 1890. English Translation. London, 1891.
MONTGERON. *La Verite des Miracles.*
MORSELLI (E TANZI). *Contributo sperimentale alla Fisiopsicologia dell' Ipnotismo.* Milan, 1889.
MOTTE. *Rapport de l'Académie Royale.* 1833.
MUSSY. *Rapport de l'Académie Royale.* 1833.
MYERS, F. W. H. *Proceedings of the Society for Psychical Research.*
OCHOROWICZ. *De la Suggestion mentale.* Paris, 1887. Translation. New York, 1890.
OSGOOD, Dr. *Boston Medical and Surgical Journal.* June 1890.
OUDET. *Rapport des Commissaires.* 1837.
PARACELSUS. *Cura Morborum Magnetica.* 1611, etc.
PELLETIER. *Rapport des Commissaires.* 1837.
PLINY. *Hist. Nat. lib. vii. and lib. xxviii.*
POISSONIER. *Rapport des Commissaires.* 1784.
POMPONATIUS. *De Incantationibus.* 1657.
RICHET, Prof. CH. *Revue Philosophique.* March 1884.
ROUX. *Rapport des Commissaires.* 1837.
SALLIN. *Rapport des Commissaires.* 1784.
SOLON. ὑποθῆκαι εἰς ἑαυτόν.
SOLOW, Dr JULIUS. *New York Medical Journal.* March 14th 1891.
SPENCER, HERBERT. *Principles of Psychology.*
STANLEY. *History of Philosophy.* 1666.
STURLURSON, SNORRO. *History of Scandinavian Kings.*
SULTONIUS. *Vespas. vii.*
THILLAYE. *Rapport de l'Académie Royale.* 1833.
TOURETTE, GILLES DE LA. *L'hypnotisme et les états analogues au point de vue médico-legal.* Paris, 1887.

TUCKEY, Dr C. LLOYD. *Psycho-Therapeutics.* 3rd ed. London, 1891. *The Value of Hypnotism in Chronic Alcoholism.* London, 1892.
TUKE, Dr HACK. *The Influence of the Mind on the Body.*
UNZER. *Beschreibung der mit dem Küntslichen Magnet angestellten Versuche.* Allina, 1775.
VAN HELMONT. *De Magnet. vuln. . . . curatione.* Paris, 1621.
VOISIN, Dr A. *Revue de l' Hypnotisme.* November 1888.
WIRDIG. *Nova Medicina Spirituum.* Hamburg, 1673.

CHAPTER I.

THE GENESIS OF HYPNOTISM.

Its early beginnings—Egypt—Greece—Rome—The Ebers Papyrus—St Justin — Asclepiades — Solon — Martial — Pliny — Tacitus — Suetonius — St Augustine — The royal touch — Paracelsus — Pomponatius—Glocenius—Kircher—Van Helmont—Digby—Maxwell — Burggrav — Wirdig — Fludd — Helinotius — Mesmer—Vienna—Hehl—Academy of Berlin—Academy of Bavaria—Dr Osterwald—Prof. Baur—Paris—Mesmer's propositions—d'Eslon—Treaties with the Academy of Science and the Royal Society of Medicine—d'Eslon and the Faculty of Medicine—The Commission of Investigation appointed—their reports—The report of Jussieu—Mesmer dies at Mörsburg—Mesmer's generosity—Defence against attacks on him.

THE science of hypnotism has been evolved from such a labyrinth of idle superstition and wild speculation that even those keenly interested in the development of human knowledge have held aloof from a subject which apparently presents so entangled a maze of insoluble riddles.

In the long course of its history it has been the frequent prey of the unscientic investigator, and indeed almost all the quacks, at one time or another, seem to have endeavoured to render it of use to them.

Its peculiar attraction for these men lay in the fact that the ordinary run of mankind knew nothing of the hypnotic state, and in the narrowness of their philosophy were wont to attribute to the supernatural or the unknowable all that their little minds could not appreciate or fathom. Many, however, of these unscientific scientists were painfully in earnest, and hypnotism was still making headway when the professional entertainer, the charlatan, the juggler, the trickster, laid their hands on the much-suffering science.

If ever men had reason to curse men, the hypnotists surely have a right to mete out the treatment to these people. No sooner had the showman's heart been gladdened by his latest "find," than he proceeded to add some "business" that his "entertainment" might be still more effective, and in a space as short in time as it was dire in its effects, hypnotism became a bye-word for all that was low and contemptible.

To those, therefore, who would have a clear knowledge of what hypnotism is and what it is not, a study of its history is a necessity; but since to many the suspension of the judgment while wading through the tale of exploded ideas may not be an easy matter, it may be well for some to read first the later chapters dealing with the modern theory of hypnotism, and then to recur to these first chapters for a more solid basis.

The history of hypnotism begins almost in fable. Methods were in use amongst the Egyptians, the

Greeks, and the Romans, which present a striking similarity to the means adopted by modern hypnotists. In the British Museum there is a bas-relief taken from a tomb in Thebes; the "subject," as he would be termed in modern phraseology, is sitting down, whilst at a short distance from him a man is standing with his hand uplifted and evidently about to "pass" over his patient. The goddess Isis on the zodiac of her temple at Denderah is represented as making these same "passes." The earliest Greek physicians were in the habit of using processes having a strong resemblance to the "cutaneous irritations" of Heidenhain.[1]

The *Ebers Papyrus*,[2] which gives us some account of the medical methods practised in Egypt prior to 1552 B.C., mentions the laying of hands on the head of the patient as a part of the treatment.

Even the "clairvoyant" theories of the Mesmerists seem to have an history, since probably the early soothsayers and oracles relied largely on the hypnotic states; and the acuteness and subtlety which the faculties often gain in deep states of hypnosis would enable the subjects to speak with a foresight and wisdom calculated to excite the admiration and reverence of those who made use of their services.

St Justin says—"The Sibyls spoke many great things with justice and truth, and that when the

---
[1] "Hypnotism." London, 1892.
[2] Dr Albert Moll (Berlin). "Hypnotism," p. 3.

instinct which animated them ceased to exist, they lost the recollection of all they had declared." Asclepiades was in the habit of putting frenzied persons to sleep by rubbing, and when these frictions were prolonged, the patient was plunged in a deep lethargy.

One of the earliest and at the same time most striking references to the use of some form of nerve stimulation as a curative agent occurs in *Solon*.[1]

"πολλάκι δ' ἐξ ὀλίγης ὀδύνης μέγα γίγνεται ἄλγος
κοὐκ ἄν τις λύσαιτ' ἤπια φάρμακα δούς
τὸν δὲ κακαῖς νούσοισι κυκώμενον ἀργαλέαις τε
ἀψάμενος χειροῖν αἶψα τίθησ' ὑγιῆ."

Martial,[2] touching apparently on some luxurious refinement, has a curious reference to the subject. Pliny[3] refers to the method, which will be described later on, of "fascination."

---

[1] "ὑποθῆκαι εἰς ἑαυτον," ll. 59-62. Stanley (*History of Philosophy*, 1666) gives the following translation:
"The smallest hurts sometimes increase and rage
More than all art of physic can assuage;
Sometime the fury of the worst disease
The hand, by gentle stroking, will appease."

[2] "Percurrit agili corpus arte tractatrix
Manumque doctam spargit omnibus membris."—Book III. Ep. 82.

[3] "Esse adjicit Isigonus, in Triballis et Illyriis qui visa quoque effascinent, interimantque quos diutius intereantur, iratis praecipue oculis: quod eorum malum praecipue sentire puberes. Notabilius esse quod pupillas binas in singulis oculis habeant. Hujus generis et feminas in Scythia, quae vocantur Bithyae, prodit Apollonides: Philarchus et in Ponto Thibiorum genus multosque alios ejusdem naturae; quorum notas tradit in altero oculo geminam pupillam in altero equi effigiem," etc. *Hist. Nat.* lib. vii. c. 2.—Pliny also recommends breathing on the forehead as a means of cure. *Hist. Nat.* lib. xxviii. c. 6.

THE GENESIS OF HYPNOTISM.

The author of the "Denarium Medicum" writes—"Fuerunt ante Hippocratem multi viri docti qui nulla prorsus medicina corporea usi sunt sed sola spiritus et animae facultate."

Tacitus [1] and Suetonius [2] testify to the cures performed by the Emperor Vespasian.

Finally, St Augustine [3] tells of a priest whom he knew and who could reduce himself to a state not to be distinguished from death.

Everyone has heard of the cures due to the "royal touch." Numerous cures were effected in this manner by the early kings of France, and the "touch" was still in vogue in Queen Anne's time. It seems to have been first exercised by the Scandinavian Princes, and particularly by St Olaf, who is supposed to have reigned from 1020 to 1035.[4] Thus we notice in various times a number of phenomena which may, at first sight, strike the reader as but distantly connected with each other; the nature and extent of their connection may be more apparent in the later chapters.

How far the Egyptians, Persians, Greeks, Romans knew of the scientific import of these phenomena and how much they knew seems impossible to decide. We have but the bare record of a number of isolated facts; there seems to be no evidence of

---

[1] Hist. iv. 81.   [2] Vespas. vii. 5, 6.
[3] *De Civitate Dei.* Migne. Patres Latini T. 41; St Aug. Vol. vii. pp. 432-3.
[4] "History of Scandinavian Kings." Snorro Sturlurson.

any common method or principle. It is not improbable, since many of the phenomena were connected with the oracles or with the most learned physicians, that the people either never took the trouble to look for any explanation, or attributed the results to supernatural agency. The first traces of any system appear towards the end of the Middle Ages, and this system grew out of the doctrines of astrology. Some of the most famous men of the day were at work on the subject, and notwithstanding the strange doctrines advocated in most of their writings, the student who ventures on them will find his time by no means lost. Prominent amongst these writers are Theophrastus Paracelsus, Petrus Pomponatius,[1] Rod. Glocenius,[2] Athanasius Kircher,[3] Van Helmont,[4] Sir Kenelm Digby,[5] Gul. Maxwell,[6] J. G. Burggrav,[7] Sebastian Wirdig,[8] and others, including Fludd and Helinotius.

[1] *De Incantationibus.* Basil, 1657.
[2] *Tract. de Magnet. vuln. curat.* Marburgi, 1608.
[3] Athanasius Kircher, S. J., one of the greatest scholars of the Middle Ages. *Magnes sive de Arte Magnetica.* Coloniae, 1643.
Magneticum Naturæ Regnum. Amst. 1667, &c., &c. For complete list of his works see "Bibliothèque de la Compagnie de Jésus." (Brussels, 1890.) See Appendix.
[4] Van Helmont. *De Magnet. Vuln. . . . curatione.* Paris 1621, &c.
[5] Sir Kenelm Digby. "Of the cure of wounds by the powder of sympathy." London, 1660.
[6] Gulielmus Maxwell. "De Medicina Magnetica." Frankf. 1679. See Appendix.
[7] J. G. Burggrav. "Cura Morborum Magnetica qua vera Theophrasti (Paracelsi?) Mumia significatur." 1611.
[8] Sebastian Wirdig. "Nova Medicina Spirituum." Hamb. 1673.

All these men, in various ways, attempted to demonstrate the existence of an universal magnetic force by which the reciprocal action of bodies, in general, upon each other, and particularly the phenomena of the human body and mind, were to be explained. The human will was capable of producing an effect upon the minds and organisms of other persons. Pomponatius and Van Helmont were the two most systematic upholders of this view. Pomponatius was Professor of Philosophy at Padua. He was born at Mantua in 1462, and died in 1525.

He sought to prove that sickness and disease were curable by means of the magnetism existing in each person. "When those who are endowed with this faculty operate by employing the force of the imagination and the will, this force affects their blood and their spirits, which produce the intended effects by means of an evaporation thrown outwards."[1]

Health, according to the same writer, may be communicated to a sick person by the same means.[2]

John Baptist van Helmont was born at Brussels in the year 1577. He was educated for the medical

---

[1] "Possibile est apud me quod homo habeat talem dispositionem qualem discimus. Sic contingit tales homines qui habeant hujusmodi vires in potentia, et per vim imaginativam et desiderativam cum actu operantur, talis virtus exit ad actum ; et afficit sanguinem et spirituum qui per evaporationem petunt ad extra et producunt tales effectus." Cap. iv. p. 44.

[2] "Incredibile non est, etiam sanitatem posse produci ad extra ab anima talitse imaginante et desiderante de aegritudine." Cap. iv. p. 51.

profession, but spent his life in chemical researches. The discovery of laudanum, of the spirit of hartshorn, and of the volatile salts are due to him; he also discovered the existence of the aëriform fluids, to which he gave the name *Gas*, a name they still retain. He died in 1644.

His book was intended partly as an answer to Glocenius, an earlier writer who had advocated the doctrines of magnetism, but not in a manner agreeable to Helmont, and partly as a reply to Fr. Robert, a Jesuit, who had contended that the cures performed by means of this magnetism were due to diabolical agency.

He makes short work of his opponents:—[1]

"Magnetism is an universal agent; there is nothing new in it but the name; and it is a paradox only to those who are disposed to ridicule everything, and who ascribe to the influence of Satan all those phenomena which they cannot explain."

He defines Magnetism as[2] "that occult power which bodies exert over each other at a distance, whether by attraction or repulsion."

Wirdig sums up his own position in few but incisive words:—"Totus mundus constat et positus est in magnetimo, omnes sublunarium vicissitudinem fiunt

---

[1] "Magnetismus, quia passim viget, praeter nomen, nil novi continet; nec paradoxus nisi iis qui cuncta derident et in Sataniae dominum ablegant quae cunque non intelligant."

[2] "Sic vocitamus eam occultam coaptationem qua absens in absens per influxum agit sive trahendo vel impellendo fiat."

THE GENESIS OF HYPNOTISM.

per magnetismum, vita conservatur magnetismo; interitus omnium rerum fiunt per magnetismum."

It is noticeable that the theories of magnetism gain force and precision in each successive writer. Paracelsus and Glocenius rather hint at than advocate the doctrine of Magnetism, but Wirdig takes up a much more decided position; whilst Maxwell's "spiritus vitalis" indicates a great development, and in fact was the legitimate precursor of Mesmer's doctrine of the "universal fluid."

It has been the fashion for modern writers to pour upon these early students little else than ridicule and contempt. From one work [1] in particular we learn that "these men wrote voluminous books, filled with sterile discussions, with unproved assertions, and with contemptible arguments."

In reply to this we can only say it is not difficult to be wise after the event. Some of the most learned men of our time are still engaged in the examination of these questions, and if the student will read the reports of the Psychical Research Society,[2] the works of Dr Hack Tuke,[3] and Dr Carpenter,[4] together with those of Kircher, Van Helmont, and others, he may find much that is curious and interesting. No doubt many of these magnetic speculations were wild, and,

---

[1] Binet et Féré, "Animal Magnetism." 3rd ed. p. 3.
[2] See Reports of Committee on Mesmerism; also papers by Myers and Gurney.
[3] "Influence of the Mind upon the Body," etc.
[4] "Mental Physiology."

no doubt, many of their methods were not altogether scientific; but the scientific method is modern, and these writers were not modern.

At this present time we are practically ignorant of the nature of that force which governs the nervous system. The blood-vessels of the body pass round the brain but they do not enter into its substance, and the brain itself is but a congerie of nerves. These nerves are light, delicate matter; what it is that gives them the power they possess we have no means of knowing.

This much we do know, that if a human body recently dead be taken, and a continuous current from a strong galvanic battery be administered, the muscles of the dead man will contract and the most violent contortions will be seen. The dead man has been known to spring upon his knees, move his head, roll his eyes, and chatter his teeth. Still more, if we take an animal and tie off the involuntary nerves that lead to the stomach, digestion will instantly cease; but on a moderate galvanic current being administered, the digestion will be immediately renewed. And between Magnetism and Electricity the difference is not striking. It seems therefore as unscientific as it is ungenerous to deny that Paracelsus and his followers, though they fell into many errors, were at any rate preparing the way for more definite and more accurate knowledge.

In the middle of the eighteenth century another

figure comes on the scene, an ardent student of the Animal Magneticians, and gifted with extraordinary talents. Friedrich Anton Mesmer was born on the banks of the Rhine, in a small town called Stein, on the 5th of May 1734. He attained his doctor's degree at Vienna, where he studied principally under Professor Van Swieten and Professor Haen. His whole life appears to have been spent in the endeavours to solve the problems which life presents; he chose for his thesis[1] on taking his degree—" The Influence of the Planets on the Human Body."

Whilst at Vienna, Mesmer seems to have been attracted still more to the whole question of Magnetism by witnessing the wonderful cures performed by

---

[1] Some writers have remarked the strangeness of such a thesis as Mesmer's being accepted. Van Swieten was world-renowned at the time, but he does not seem to have been altogether orthodox, if we may judge from the following title page of a book dedicated to him:—
" Androphili Asclepiadei Liber, in quo pauca explicantur, quorum scitu sanitas conservari et vita Hominis, *ab ignorantia medicorum* poterit esse secura." Neostadii in Austria, 1747.

The Editor's name does not appear, but the *Imprimatur* given by the Bishop is interesting, and shows the esteem in which Van Swieten was held at the time:—"Cum praesens opusculum cui titulus: 'Androphili Asclepiadei liber, in quo pauca explicantur, quorum scitu sanitas conservari et vita hominis ab ignorantia medicorum poterit esse secura'; nihil contineat, quod Fidei Orthodoxæ aut bonis moribus adversetur, imo a Clarissimo Viro, Gerh. van Swieten Sacrae Caesareae Regiaeque Majestatis Archiatro pulcherrimo exornatum fit encomio; hinc non tantum facultatem damus, ut prelo mandetur, sed et dignissimum censemus, quod in lucem prodeat. In quorum fidem, etc. Datae Neostadii in Austria ex Curia Episcopali die 23. Junii, Anno 1747.—FERDINANDUS EPISCOPUS."

Father Hehl,[1] a Jesuit. These cures were supposed to be due to the subtle influence or fluid of magnetism, which was imparted to the patients from steel plates and magnets specially prepared for the purpose.[2]

Having investigated the matter, and having satisfied himself of the genuineness of the cures, he entered upon a series of independent experiments. Chance discovered what he could not. On one

---

[1] Maximilian Hehl, Professor of Astronomy at Vienna, was born at Chemnitz in Hungary in the year 1720. During the year 1745 and 1746 he assisted Father J. Francois, the head of the Jesuits' observatory at Vienna. He then went to Clausenberg in Transilvania to teach mathematics, and was recalled some years afterwards to Vienna, where he became the chief astronomer. From 1757 to 1786 he published yearly Ephemerides. At the request of Count Bachoff (the Danish Ambassador at Vienna), he set out for Lapland in April 1768 to observe the transit of Venus, and having accomplished his object, returned to Vienna in 1770. He died on the 14th of April 1792. Amongst his works are:—

"Tabulae Solares N. L. de la Caille, cum suppl. reliquar tabular." 1763.

"Tabulae lunares Tob. Mayer. cum suppl. W. Cassini de Lalande, et suis." 1763.

"De transitu Veneris ante discum solis die tertio," Jun. 1769; Wardachusii in Finmarchia observato, 1770. "De Paralaxi solis ex observatione transitus, Veneris anni, 1769, 1773," etc.

[2] Upon the value of the mineral magnet in the cure of sickness and disease numerous early authors had written. Its use seems to have been recommended by Galen and Dioscorides. The following are some of the chief works:—

Ludwig. "Dissert. de Magnetismo in corpore humano." Leips. 1772.

Unzer. "Beschreibung der mit dem Küntslichen Magnet angestellten Versuche." Altona, 1775.

Heinsius. "Beyträge zu meinen Versuchen welche mit künstlichen Magneten in verschiedenen Krankheiten angestellt worden." Leips. 1776. "Sammlung der neusten gedruckten und geschriebenen Nachrichten von Magnetcuren." Leips. 1778. "Historia Trismitonici quadraginta fere septimarum a Philiatro de Wocher curati." Freiburg, 1778.

occasion Mesmer had bled a patient, and was getting the magnetic tractors to heal the wound, when he accidentally passed his hand over the cicatrix, and was astonished to find that the pass of his hand had done what had hitherto been effected only by means of the magnets.

This shed a new light on the phenomena, and in 1775 Mesmer issued a circular letter, addressed, in the first place, to the leading academies. In this he maintained the existence of Animal Magnetism by means of which men could mentally influence each other, and he drew a strong distinction between the magnetism which he termed animal and the magnetism of metals. The Academy of Berlin was the only one that replied to his letter, and its answer was not favourable.

About this time, however, the Academy of Bavaria nominated him as a member. The publication of reports of Mesmer's cases in the newspapers roused Vienna to a high pitch of excitement. One of the directors of the Academy of Science at Munich, a Dr Osterwald, said that he had been cured of paralysis; another Professor, named Baur, stated that he had been completely cured of ophthalmia. Not only the people but the court were to be seen at his levées and his seances. Mesmer at first cured only by contact, but he put forward later the theory that various objects of iron, wood, etc., were capable of receiving the necessary magnetism, and he used in consequence various mechanical means for the conveyance of the fluid.

Vienna had indeed been roused by Mesmer's work, but from the first he was the object of great enmity. This hostility was due largely to the vested interests of the faculty which seemed at stake; but Mesmer himself was anything but conciliatory, and in 1778 he left Vienna and went to Paris.

Binet and Féré[1] state that, "obliged to quit Vienna, in consequence of some adventure not clearly explained, Mesmer came to Paris." This rumour of some scandalous adventure seems to have been industriously circulated by Mesmer's many enemies as his reason for leaving Vienna, till by its constant repetition it gained general credence. I have been unable to find any authority for the "adventure not clearly explained," and there seems no reason to suppose that the cause of his leaving was anything more than the general hostility manifested against him. In Paris, Mesmer constructed his famous "baquet" or tub. This seems to have been a wonderful piece of apparatus. Deleuze describes it as follows:—

"In the centre of a large room stood an oak tub, four or five feet in diameter and one foot deep; it was closed by a lid made in two pieces and enclosed in another tub or bucket. At the bottom of the tub a number of bottles were laid in convergent rows

[1] Op. cit. p. 4.

so that the neck of each bottle turned towards the centre. Other bottles filled with magnetised water, tightly corked down, were laid in divergent rows with their necks turned outwards. Several rows were thus piled up, and the apparatus was then said to be at 'high pressure.' The tub was filled with water, to which was sometimes added powdered glass and iron filings. There were also some dry tubs, that is, prepared in the same manner, but without any additional water. The lid was perforated to allow of the passage of moveable bent-iron rods, which could be applied to the different parts of the patients' bodies. A long rope was also fastened to a ring in the lid, and the patients placed this loosely round their limbs. No diseases offensive to the sight, such as sores, wens, or deformities, were healed. The patients then drew near to each other, touching hands, arms, knees, or feet. The handsomest, youngest, and most robust magnetisers held also an iron rod, with which they touched the dilatory or refractory patients. The rods and ropes had all undergone a preparation, and in a very short space of time the patients felt the magnetic influence. The women, being the most easily affected, were almost at once seized with fits of yawning and stretching, their eyes closed, their legs gave way, and they seemed to suffocate. In vain did musical glasses and harmonies resound, the piano and voices re-echo, these supposed aids only seemed to increase the patients' convulsive movements. Sardonic laughter, piteous moans, and torrents of tears burst forth on all sides. The bodies were thrown back in spasmodic jerks, the respirations sounded like death rattles, the most terrifying symptoms were exhibited. Then suddenly the actors of this strange scene would frantically or rapturously rush towards each other, either rejoicing and embracing or thrusting away their neighbours with every appearance of horror.

"Another room was padded, and presented a different spectacle. There, women beat their heads against the padded walls or rolled on the cushion-covered floor in fits of suffocation. In the midst of this panting, quivering throng, Mesmer, dressed in a lilac coat, moved about, extending a magic wand towards the least suffering, halting in front of the most violently excited and gazing steadily into their eyes, while he held both their hands in his, bringing the middle fingers in immediate contact, to establish the communication. At another moment he would, by a motion of open hands and extended fingers, operate with the 'great current,' crossing and uncrossing his arms with wonderful rapidity to make the final passes." Bailly, who was later the reporter to one of the scientific commissions which were appointed to examine the Mesmeric theories, was a witness of these scenes, and he also has left an account of them. The year 1779 is important as the one in which Mesmer published a paper,[1] claim-

[1] Memoire sur la découverte du Magnétisme animal. Paris, 1779.

ing that he had discovered a principle capable of curing every disease. He sums up in twenty-seven propositions :—

1. There is a reciprocal action and reaction between the planets, the earth, and animate nature.
2. The means by which this influence acts and reacts is a fluid universally diffused, so continuous as not to admit of a break, incomparably subtle and susceptible of receiving, increasing, and communicating all motor disturbances.
3. This reciprocal action is subject to mechanical but as yet unknown laws.
4. The reciprocal effects resulting from this action may be considered as flux and reflux.
5. This reflux is more or less general, more or less special, more or less complex, according to the nature of the causes which determine it.
6. It is by this action, the most universal which occurs in nature, that the exercise of active relations between the planets, the earth and its constituent parts, takes place.
7. The properties of matter and of organic substance depend on this action.
8. The animal body experiences the reciprocal effects of this agent, and is directly affected by its insinuation into the substance of the nerves.
9. Properties are displayed analogous to those of the magnet, particularly in the human body,

in which diverse and opposite poles are likewise to be distinguished, and these may be communicated, changed, destroyed, and reinforced. Even the phenomenon of declination may be observed.

10. This property of the human body, which renders it susceptible of the influence of the planets and of the reciprocal action of those which environ it, manifests its analogy with the magnet, and this has led me to adopt the term " animal magnetism."
11. The action and virtue of animal magnetism, thus characterised, may be communicated to other bodies inanimate or animate.
12. This action and virtue may be strengthened and diffused by such bodies.
13. Experiments show that there is a diffusion of matter, subtle enough to penetrate all bodies without any considerable loss of energy.
14. Its action takes place at a remote distance, without the aid of any intermediary substance.
15. It is, like light, increased and reflected by mirrors.
16. It is communicated, propagated, and increased by sound.
17. This magnetic virtue may be accumulated, concentrated, and transported.
18. I have said that animated bodies are not all equally susceptible; in a few instances they possess so opposite a property that their presence

is sufficient to destroy all the effects of magnetism upon other bodies.
19. This opposite virtue likewise penetrates all bodies; it also may be communicated, propagated, accumulated, concentrated, and transported, reflected by mirrors, and propagated by sound. This does not merely constitute a negative, but a positive opposite virtue.
20. The magnet, whether natural or artificial, is like other bodies susceptible of animal magnetism, and even of the opposite virtue; in neither case does its action on fire or on the needle suffer any change, and this shows that the principle of animal magnetism essentially differs from that of mineral magnetism.
21. This system sheds new light upon the nature of fire and of light, as well as on the theory of attraction, of flux and reflux, of the magnet and of electricity.
22. It teaches us that the magnet and artificial electricity have, with respect to diseases, properties common to a host of other agents presented to us by nature, and that if the use of these has been attended by some useful results, they are due to animal magnetism.
23. These facts show, in accordance with the practical rules I am about to establish, that this principle will cure nervous diseases directly, and other diseases indirectly.

24. By its aid the physician is enlightened as to the use of medicine, and may render its action more perfect, and he can provoke and direct salutary crises so as to have them completely under his control.
25. In communicating my method, I shall, by a new theory of matter, demonstrate the universal utility of the principle I seek to establish.
26. Possessed of this knowledge, the physician may judge with certainty of the origin, nature, and progress of diseases, however complicated they may be; he may hinder their development and accomplish their cure without exposing the patient to dangerous and troublesome consequences, irrespective of age, temperament, and sex. Even women in a state of pregnancy and during parturition may reap the same advantage.
27. This doctrine will finally enable the physician to decide upon the health of every individual, and of the presence of the diseases to which he may be exposed. In this manner the art of healing may be brought to absolute perfection.

The temporary success at Vienna seemed likely to be turned into a lasting one at Paris. Not only did many physicians of good standing and many intelligent men proclaim their adherence to his theories, but both pupils and patients were flocking to him in large and increasing numbers. His triumph appeared assured when he made a convert of one of the greatest scientists of the day—d'Eslon, the first physician to the Comte d'Artois. So great were the demands made on him that Mesmer soon found it necessary to employ several assistants. It must be mentioned that the crises to which Deleuze refers were regarded by Mesmer as an important feature, and unless these could be excited, the cure was doubtful.

There seems but little doubt that these crises were no more and no less than hysterical attacks brought about by the exciting combination of circumstances. Expectant attention, combined with the strange scenes in which they were taking part, would be sufficient to induce such a state in many who were not subject to hysteria; whilst when one had been affected in this manner the infection would rapidly spread. Mesmer at first had taken up his abode in the Place Vendôme, but his house there was soon too small to accommodate the patients, and his next step was to purchase the Hôtel Bullion, where he established four separate *baquets;* one of these he reserved for the poor, whom he treated gratuitously. This provision, however, was insufficient, and he then magnetised a tree in the Rue Bondy, where thousands of the sick poor were to be seen connected to the tree in the hope of cure—a hope, under these altered circumstances, but seldom realised.

Mesmer had asked the Academy of Science and

the Royal Society of Medicine to institute an enquiry into his treatment, but he would not assent to the rigorous conditions laid down by these bodies. He wished them to attend his seances and witness his experiments, and would hear of nothing else. Neither would agree to the terms of the other, and angry recrimination was all that came of Mesmer's attempt to obtain a Committee of Investigation.

The Faculty of Medicine, at d'Eslon's request, summoned a general meeting to examine his statements and Mesmer's propositions. The meeting was extremely hostile, and the Faculty, without troubling to examine the question or to discuss the facts, threatened to erase d'Eslon's name from the list of physicians unless he withdrew from his position. Nothing could have been more unfair or more unscientific than this action on the part of the Faculty; and Mesmer's unwillingness to submit his theories, without reserve, to the examination of these men seems justified by the events which followed.

At d'Eslon's instigation, Mesmer published a paper,[1] as a vindication of himself against the monstrously unfair attacks made upon him at the time. The prejudice was so great that the censors allowed no article to appear in the newspapers which had emanated from any of his partisans.

Disgusted with the bigotry and intolerance of

[1] "Precis historique des faits relatifs au magnétisme animal." Paris, 1781.

THE GENESIS OF HYPNOTISM. 23

the medical profession, he left Paris, and absolutely refused to stay, though the Government offered him a life pension of 20,000 francs if he would remain. But his pupils besought him to return, and in response to their request he came back and gave a course of lectures. Success still seemed possible, when bitterness, rivalry, and jealousy divided his followers, and he found himself attacked from within as well as from without. Nothing was certain, and every one seemed to be engaged in defending or attacking the theories which Mesmer had propounded, when the Government made an attempt to secure some sort of peace and certainty by appointing a commission in 1874 to report upon the whole question. There were in fact two commissions. The one, composed of members of the Faculty of Medicine, of the Academy of Sciences, and some well-known men, such as Franklin and Lavoisier; the other taken from the members of the Royal Society of Medicine. The reports of both were unfavourable to Mesmer's claims. The two commissions presented elaborate reports, giving a detailed account of their meetings and experiments. Owing to their great length it is impossible to quote them in full but as it is necessary that the reader should have a clear view of the nature of the questions in dispute, and of the position assumed by the various scientists of the time, the conclusions are given below.

The student will find the full text in the printed reports published, and a valuable historical commentary on this is supplied by the work [1] of Burdin and Dubois, which also contains the reports of the later commissions.

The commission of the Academy of Science was the first to publish its report, and its conclusion is as follows:—[2]

"The commissioners have ascertained that the animal magnetic fluid is not perceptible by any of the senses; that it has no action, either on themselves or on the patients subjected to it. They are convinced that pressure and contact effect changes which are rarely favourable to the animal system, and which injuriously affect the imagination. Finally they have demonstrated by decisive experiments that imagination, apart from magnetism, produces convulsions, and that magnetism without imagination produces nothing. They have come to the unanimous conclusion with respect to the existence and utility of magnetism, that there is nothing to prove the existence of the animal fluid; that this fluid, since it is non-existent, has no beneficial effects; that the violent effects observed in patients

[1] Histoire Académique du Magnétisme Animal accompagnée de notes et de remarques critiques sur toutes les observations et experiences faites jusqu'a ce jour par C. Burdin, *Jeune* et Fréd. Dubois (d'Amiens). Paris, 1841.

[2] Rapport des Commissaires de la faculté de Medecine et de l'académie des Sciences chargés par le Roi de l'examen du Magnétisme animal. Paris, 1784.

under public treatment are due to contact, to the excitement of imagination, and to the mechanical imitation which involuntarily impels us to repeat that which strikes our senses. At the same time, they are compelled to add, since it is an important observation, that the contact and repeated excitement of the imagination which produced the crises may become hurtful; that the spectacle of these crises is likewise dangerous, on account of the imitative faculty, which is a law of nature; and consequently that all treatment in public in which magnetism is employed must in the end be productive of evil results."

    (Signed) " B. FRANKLIN, MAJAULT, LE ROY, SALLIN, BAILLY, D'ARCET, DE BORY, GUILLOTIN, LAVOISIER."

" PARIS, 11*th of August* 1784."

From the report it will be seen that the commissioners considered the imagination responsible for the phenomena they had been appointed to examine, and denied altogether the existence of the force to which Mesmer had given the name animal magnetism.

In addition to this public report the commissioners presented a private report to the king, in which they referred to the objectionable features of the seances, and insisted strongly on the moral danger of the practice of animal magnetism.

The Royal Society of Medicine issued their report on the 16th of August, and their conclusions agreeing in the main with that of the Academy of Sciences and the Faculty of Medicine were as follows [1] :—

It follows from the first part of our report—

1. That the so-called *animal magnetism*, as it has been put forth in our days, is an ancient system, praised in past centuries, and then forgotten.
2. That the advocates of animal magnetism, either those who invented this system or those who have revived it amongst us, have not been able in the past, nor can they now give any proof of the existence of the unknown agent, or of "the fluid" to which they have ascribed certain powers and effects, and that consequently the existence of this agent is gratuitously assumed.
3. That what has been called *animal magnetism*, reduced to its proper value by the examination and analysis of facts, is the art of causing to fall into convulsions by the touching of the most irritable parts of the body, and by the friction exercised on these parts, very sensitive persons, after they have been prepared for this result by multiplied and concomitant causes,

[1] Rapport des Commissaires de la Société Royale de Medecine. Paris, 1784.

which can be varied at will, and of which some alone are capable of producing most violent convulsions in certain cases and in certain subjects

4. We have begun the second part of our report by remarking that if the *so-called animal magnetism* vaunted in the last century had really been useful, the use of it would have been established and perpetuated.

5. We have shown that it is by an error in the use of terms that the effects produced by *animal magnetism* have been called *crises;* that between these which are the means nature employs to heal, and the effects of the so-called magnetism, there is no relationship except in the similarity of names, whilst all the essential and constituent conditions are diametrically opposed.

6. We have detailed the numerous and serious dangers to which we are exposed by the use of the *so-called animal magnetism;* we have insisted on the evil effects which are to be feared from the convulsions it excites and the evacuations it causes.

Consequently we are of opinion—

1. That the theory of *animal magnetism* is a system absolutely without proof.
2. That this so-called method of healing, reduced to the irritation of sensitive parts, to imagination

and its effects, is at least useless to those in whom neither evacuations nor convulsions follow, and that it may become dangerous by provoking and carrying to a too high degree the tension of fibres in those whose nerves are highly sensitive.

3. That it is very harmful to those in whom it produces effects which have been wrongly called *crises;* that it is all the more dangerous as the so-called *crises* are stronger or the convulsions more violent and the evacuations more abundant, and that there are many natures in whom the consequences may be fatal.

4. That the treatment in public by the process of *animal magnetism* adds to all the drawbacks mentioned above that of exposing a large number of otherwise well-constituted persons to contract a spasmodic or convulsive habit, which may become the source of the greatest evils.

5. That these conclusions must extend to all that is now presented to the public under the name of *animal magnetism,* since the apparatus and effects being everywhere the same, the inconvenience and dangers to which it exposes persons deserve everywhere the same attention.

(Signed) POISSONIER, CAILLE,
MANDUYT, ANDRY.

PARIS, 16*th of August* 1784.

These reports, however conclusive they might otherwise have been, were practically nullified by the withdrawal of Laurent de Jussieu, the great botanist, from the commission of the Royal Society of Medicine. Jussieu had admittedly examined the experiments with extraordinary care and thoroughness, and found himself in consequence unable to agree with his colleagues. He published a separate report with the object of showing that he had produced certain effects which could not be explained by imagination; and he stated, as the result of his observations, that a sensible action was produced by friction, by contact, and even by proximity. He did not adopt the term animal magnetism, but attributed the influence to "animal heat," or as he termed it later, "animalised electric fluid."

He discussed the subject elaborately in this report [1] which he issued, and his examination was most thorough and scientific. It must suffice here to give his conclusion.

"*Conclusion.*—The theory of magnetism cannot be admitted until it is developed and supported by solid proof. The experiments made to verify the existence of the magnetic fluid only prove that man produces a sensible action on his fellow by friction, by contact, and more rarely by the mere fact of

[1] Rapport de l'un des commissaires chargés par le Roi de l'examen du magnétisme animal. Paris, 1784.

drawing nearer. This action, attributed to a non-established universal fluid, certainly belongs to the animal heat in bodies, which continually emanates from them, goes sufficiently far, and can pass from one body into another. Animal heat is developed, increased, or diminished in a body by causes either mental or physical; judged by its effects, it shares the properties of tonic medicines, and produces like them effects either good or bad according to the dose and the circumstances under which it is used. A widespread and more intelligent use of this agent will better show its real action and degree of utility. Every doctor may follow the methods he considers advantageous to the treatment of diseases, but on condition that he publishes his methods when they are new or opposed to the ordinary practice. Those who have established, spread, or followed the treatment known as magnetic, and who propose to continue, are therefore bound to reveal their observations and discoveries; and we must proscribe any such treatment the process of which shall not be made known by prompt publication."

"A. L. DE JUSSIEU."

Mesmer had been with difficulty induced to return to Paris. After the report of the commissions, there seemed little temptation for him to remain, and he returned to Germany.

He died and was buried in Mörsburg in 1815.

The Berlin physicians erected a monument over the grave in honour of his memory.

It has been the fashion to sneer at him, and to accuse him especially of avarice.

We can hardly reconcile Mesmer's treatment of the poor with avarice, and his kindness does not seem to have been limited to these.

Deleuze relates that M. Nicolas, a physician of Grenoble, was one of those who came to be enrolled among his pupils. Having paid down the sum required, he confessed that the sacrifice embarrassed him a good deal. "I thank you, sir," said Mesmer, "for your zeal and confidence; but, my dear brother, don't let this make you uneasy. Here are an hundred louis; carry them to the box, that it may be believed you have paid as well as the rest; and let this remain a secret between ourselves."

We cannot do better than quote the words of Dr Moll[1] of Berlin :—

"I do not wish to join the contemptible group of Mesmer's professional slanderers. He is dead and can no longer defend himself from those who disparage him without taking into consideration the circumstances or the time in which he lived.

"Against the universal opinion that he was avaricious, I remark that in Vienna, as well as later in Mörsburg and Paris, he always helped the poor without reward. I believe that he erred in his

[1] "Hypnotism," p. 6.

teaching, but think it is just to attack this only, and not his personal character. Mesmer was much slandered in his lifetime, and these attacks upon him have been continued till quite lately. Let us, however, consider more closely in what his alleged great crime consisted. He believed in the beginning that he could heal by means of a magnet, and later, that he could do so by means of a personal indwelling force which he could transfer to the *baquet*. This was evidently his firm belief, and he never made a secret of it. Others believed that the patient's mere imagination played a part, or that Mesmer produced his effects by some concealed means. Then, by degrees, arose the legend that Mesmer possessed some secret by means of which he was able to produce effects on people, such as the cure of diseases, but that he would not reveal it. In reality the question was not at all of a secret purposely kept back by him, since he imagined and always insisted that he exercised some individual force. Finally, if he used this supposititious individual force for the purpose of earning money, he did nothing worse than do modern physicians' and proprietors of institutions who likewise do not follow their calling from pure love of their neighbour, but seek to earn their own living by it, as they are quite justified in doing. Mesmer did not behave worse than those who nowadays discover a new drug and regard the manufacture of it as a means of enriching themselves.

THE GENESIS OF HYPNOTISM. 33

Let us at last be just, and cease to slander Mesmer, who did only what is done by the people just mentioned. That those who defame Mesmer know the least about his teaching, and have the least acquaintance with his works, is very clearly shown by a whole series of books about modern hypnotism."

It seems ever the habit of the shallow scientist to plume himself on the more accurate theories which have been provided for him by the progress of knowledge and of science, and then having been fed with a limited historical *pabulum*, to turn and talk lightly, and with an air of the most superior condescension, of the weaknesses and follies of those but for whose patient labours our modern theories would probably be non-existent.[1]

[1] Besides those already quoted, the following are some of the chief publications of the period on the subject:—

"Supplement aux deux rapports de MM. les commissaires de l'académie et de la faculté de médecine et de la société royale de médecine." Anon., Paris, 1784.

"C'est la réponse la plus sage et la plus concluante qu'on ait faite aux rapports; elle est rédigée avec une extrême clarté. Il n'y a aucune idée systematique : on n'y aperçoit pas la moindre trace d'exagération ou d'enthousiasme. Je suis surpris qu'elle n'ait pas fait plus de sensation. Il me paroit qu'elle suffit pour démontrer à tout esprit droit l'injustice des attaques dirigées contre le magnétisme et l'efficacité de cet agent." Deleuze. "Histoire Critique du Magnétisme animal." Part ii., p. 59.

"Considérations sur le Magnétisme animal sur la théorie du monde et des êtres organisés," par M. Bergasse. La Haye, 1784.

"La Colosse aux pieds d'argile," par M. Wevillers. 1784.

This is a very cleverly written sketch, and exposes the commission to much keen sarcasm.

"Traité théorique et pratique du Magnétisme animal," par M. Doppet, docteur en médecine de la faculté de Turin. 1784.

"Observations sur le Magnétisme animal," par M. d'Eslon. Paris, 1780.

"Lettre de M. d'Eslon, docteur-régent de la faculté de médecine de Paris, premier médecin de monseigneur le comte d'Artois ; à M. Philip, doyen en charge de la même faculté." La Haye, 1782.

"Lettre sur le Magnétisme animal, ou l'on examine la conformité des opinions des peuples anciens et modernes, des savants et notamment de M. Bailly, avec celle de M. Mesmer et où l'on compare ses mêmes opinions au rapport des commissaires" ; adressée à M. Bailly de l'académie des sciences," etc., par M. Galard de Montjoye. Paris, 1784.

"Doutes d'un provincial, proposés à MM. les médecins-commissaires," etc. Lyon, 1784.

The author, according to Deleuze, was M. Servan, "ancien avocat-général au parlement de Grenoble."

"Analyse raisonné des rapports des commissaires," etc., par J. Bonnefoy, membre du collège royal de chirurgie de Lyon. Lyon, 1784.

"Réflexions impartiales sur le Magnétisme animal, faites après la publication du rapport de MM. les commissaires." 1784.

CHAPTER II.

THE LATER HISTORY OF HYPNOTISM.

Puységur—Buzancy—Pététin—The Abbé Faria—Deleuze—Germany—Dr Wolfart—Bertrand—Noizet—Du Potet—Georget—Rostan—Foissac—New commission appointed—Their report—Further commission and its report—Burdin *jeune*—Pigeaire—Resolution of the Academy of Science—Schopenhauer—The abuses of magnetism—Père Lacordaire—Du Potet—Elliotson—Braid—La Fontaine—Braid's experiments—Azam—Liébault—Dumont—Charcot—Bernheim—Nancy—Beaunis—Liégois—The two schools of hypnotism—Its progress—Kingsbury—Bramwell—Tuckey—Myers—Gurney—Encyclical to all the Bishops—The morality of hypnotism.

THE previous chapter was an attempt to give a brief sketch of the historical aspect of Animal Magnetism till the time when Mesmer ceased to take a prominent part in its advocacy. It is extremely difficult to know where to draw the line between a bare outline of the facts and a critical discussion of the various questions raised; but the latter would seem to be out of place here, and I must content myself with hoping that at some future time I may be able to deal more accurately with this interesting part of the subject. The question was not allowed to drop with the retirement of Mesmer; but, on the contrary, the greatest interest was manifested in the experiments and observations of his disciples. Prominent amongst these was the Marquis Chastenet de Puységur. Many causes tended towards the progress of magnetism in his hands. It must be admitted that Mesmer had made extremely rash and inconsiderate attacks on every one who would not forthwith join him; and in addition to this unfortunate propensity he seemed to be imbued with an innate love of the mysterious; whilst he must have displeased many who might otherwise have been attached to him, by his sensational manner of procedure.

None of these faults were present in de Puységur. At Buzancy, he lived on his estate a quiet and retired life, contenting himself with his experiments, and curing those whom he could.

To him is due the discovery of the hypnotic stage known as "somnambulism," a condition many fall into, under hypnosis, and in which the most striking experiments may be performed. It will be referred to more fully when discussing the various forms of hypnosis.

De Puységur, as was very natural under the circumstances, wrongly interpreted many of the strange characteristics of this state. At that time the power of the subject to receive "unconscious suggestion" was not known, and, indeed, remained unknown for some long time after.

Ignorance of this led the Marquis to conclude that

in the somnambulic state "thought transference," "clairvoyance," and other impossible powers were to be found in the subject.

De Puységur seems to have thought that Mesmer knew of this state, and Dr Moll,[1] whilst admitting that it is doubtful, inclines to the opinion that Mesmer was aware of it. It is difficult to suppose that in the thousands of cases which came under Mesmer's notice there were no patients who fell into the state of somnambulism; at the same time, Mesmer thoroughly believed that his own personal and mental influence was a most important factor, and this, with him, might easily have accounted for the phenomena common to the state. It seems quite possible that the idea of a stage, distinct and *sui generis*, never occurred to him.

De Puységur apparently first identified the state in a peasant who was suffering from inflammation of the lungs. The peasant, by name Victor, was thrown into a quiet sleep free from the convulsions which had generally attended the induction of the state. It was found that he could be made cheerful or sad, to sing or to dance in accordance with the suggestion conveyed to him by the operator.

Guided by the new knowledge, de Puységur at once proceeded to look for similar cases, and to his great delight found many. This time Buzancy was the rendezvous of all the sick; they came in their

[1] Op. cit., p. 7.

numbers, and the quiet, humble Marquis soon found himself at his wit's end to know how to attend to the wants of all his patients. The scientific world was better represented than it had been with Mesmer, and it is related that at Buzancy the patients were to be seen quite free from the terrible convulsions and fits which Mesmer induced, enjoying a peaceful and refreshing sleep.[1]

The number of patients increased so rapidly that the plan of Mesmer was resorted to, and de Puységur magnetised an elm which was widely known as "Puységur's tree." In this case the operator, however, was frequently in attendance, and many cures were effected.

Mesmer's pupil was still a very long way from the truth, but he had made a great advance on his master's system. It is admitted by all that de Puységur was as honest as the day, and no doubt much of the real impression which he created was due to his quiet, disinterested, and more scientific efforts.

It can be easily understood, however, that the super-normal element of the somnambulic stage, which entered into de Puységur's theory, presented great scope for the professional entertainers, of which they were by no means too slow to avail themselves, and the silly and the credulous were greatly imposed upon by these charlatans, who invented the most

[1] Détails des cures opérées à Buzancy. Cloquet. Soissons, 1784.

ridiculous theories, and succeeded in disgusting most sober-minded people. In a large number of semi-educated communities a rage started for the formation of societies devoted to the study and practice of magnetism. They generally took the name of Harmonic Societies, and under their auspices untold wonders were performed *ad libitum*. Pététin's name must be mentioned in passing. He was President of the Medical Society at Lyons, and strongly opposed all the theories of Mesmer. He is noticeable as having been the first to publish an account of the phenomena known as "transposition of the senses." He brought before the Lyons Society a woman, who, according to his account, could see, hear, feel, smell, and taste by means of the stomach, and also by means of her fingers; several observations of a like nature were made by him. It is still a point of controversy whether this transposition is a physical fact or whether it is due to suggestion, and the increased faculties of the person hypnotised; they who maintain the actual transposition of the senses are, however, very few, and there seems little doubt that it falls under the category of suggestive faculties (see Chap. V). In 1813 a very striking development, in reality the first sign of a distinct break from the ideas of Mesmer, was introduced by the Abbé Faria who came from India. He claimed, perhaps indefinitely, and with no very clear perception of the change from the waking to the sleeping state, that the hypnotic sleep was due not to magnetism or to any influence possessed by the operator, but to physiological action on the brain—that, in fact, it depended not on the hypnotist, but on the subject. In this year, too, Deleuze published his valuable work on the history of Animal Magnetism.[1]

The advocacy of the magnetic doctrines had not been confined to Paris, though the ever-varying course of its fortunes there claims most of the historian's attention. As early as the year 1785 Animal Magnetism had gained ground in Germany.

Throughout, the enquiry was of a much more thorough and scientific nature than at Paris; so much so, that the foremost physicians were lecturing at the Universities on the subject. In France, the study of magnetism had been practically left to laymen, and the natural results of such negligence were soon apparent; in Germany the opposite was the case, and many scientists were engaged in its investigation. By 1800 it had spread to practically every country, and was received in Denmark and Russia with much enthusiasm.

The Prussian Government (1812) commissioned Dr Wolfart to visit Mesmer and report on the subject. He returned a zealous supporter of Mag-

---

[1] Histoire critique du Magnétisme animal. J. P. F. Deleuze. 2 vols. Paris, 1813.

netism, using it in his treatment, and lecturing on the subject at the Berlin University.

In all these countries, however, Magnetism led a quiet, sober, and respectable life. The sturdy Teuton took magnetism as he takes most things—quietly. Not so with the French; there, one was a magnetist or not a magnetist, a believer or not a believer; it must have been the *bête noire* of every patient investigator. Dr Bertrand, in 1820, gave a series of public lectures on the old theme, and General Noizet prepared a paper for the Royal Academy at Berlin; in both of these there is evidence that the Abbé Faria's experiments and observations had not been without effect, though neither Bertrand nor Noizet had been able to free themselves from the current theories, and their contributions to the question are of little value. Till the governors of the hospitals put an end to them, Du Potet, Georget, and Rostan were carrying out experiments at the Hôtel-Dieu and the Salpêtrière. Foissac endeavoured to persuade the Academy of Medicine to take up the question again, relying chiefly on the fact that Laurent de Jussieu had broken at the time with the commission of 1784, and had published the report which has been mentioned in the first chapter. Foissac eventually succeeded in gaining the hearing of the Academy, and they appointed a committee to decide whether a further examination of Animal Magnetism were necessary or expedient. The committee reported in favour of a commission being appointed, and in June 1825 a commission of eleven was nominated. The commission seemed to be in no hurry, and it was only after five years' research that in June 1831 they presented their report.[1]

The report is valuable on account of the very good description of some of the states which it gives, and for this reason, I append the conclusions of the report in full. A very careful and detailed account of the various experiments made preceded these conclusions.

CONCLUSIONS.

1. The contact of the thumbs or of the hands; frictions, or certain gestures which are made, at a small distance from the body, and called *passes*, are the means employed to place ourselves in magnetic connection; or, in other words, to transmit the magnetic influence to the patient.
2. The means which are external and visible are not always necessary, since on many occasions the will, the fixed look, have been found sufficient to

---

[1] The Academy were afraid to print this report, and consequently no official text is in existence. The conclusions are taken from "Rapport et Discussions de l'Academie Royale, sur le Magnétisme animal." M. P. Foissac. Paris, 1833. A translation of the report, made by J. C. Colquhoun (Edin. 1833), says that it was taken from a lithographed copy supplied to the members of the Academy. Husson, also, published later a work containing the report of the commission and an account of their meetings.

produce the magnetic phenomena, even without the knowledge of the patient.

3. Magnetism has taken effect upon persons of different sex and age.
4. The time required for transmitting the magnetic influence with effect has varied from half-an-hour to a minute.
5. In general, magnetism does not act upon persons in a sound state of health.
6. Neither does it act upon all sick persons.
7. Sometimes during the process of magnetising there are manifested insignificant and evanescent effects which cannot be attributed to magnetism alone; such as a slight degree of oppression of heat or of cold, and some other nervous phenomena, which can be explained, without the intervention of a particular agent, upon the principle of hope or of fear, prejudice, and the novelty of the treatment, the *ennui* produced by the monotony of the gestures, the silence and repose in which the experiments are made; finally, by the imagination, which has so much influence on some minds and on certain organisations.
8. A certain number of the effects observed appeared to us to depend on magnetism alone, and were never produced without its application. These are well-established physiological and therapeutic phenomena.

9. The real effects produced by magnetism are very various. It agitates some and soothes others. Most commonly, it occasions a momentary acceleration of the respiration and of the circulation, fugitive fibrillary convulsive motions resembling electric shocks, a numbness in a greater or less degree, heaviness, somnolency, and in a small number of cases that which the magnetisers call somnambulism.
10. The existence of an uniform character to enable us to recognise, in every case, the reality of the state of somnambulism has not been established.
11. However, we may conclude with certainty that this state exists, when it gives rise to the development of new faculties, which have been designated by the names of *clairvoyance, intuition, internal prevision*, or when it produces great changes in the physical economy, such as insensibility, a sudden and considerable increase of strength, and when these effects cannot be referred to any other cause.
12. As among the effects attributed to somnambulism there are some which may be feigned; somnambulism itself may be feigned, and furnish quackery with the means of deception. Thus in the observation of these phenomena which do not present themselves again, but as isolated facts, it is only by means of the most attentive

scrutiny, the most rigid precautions and numerous and varied experiments, that we can escape illusion.

13. Sleep produced with more or less promptitude is a real but not a constant effect of magnetism.
14. We hold it as demonstrated that it has been produced in circumstances in which the persons could not see, or were ignorant of, the means employed to occasion it.
15. When a person has once been made to fall into the magnetic sleep, it is not always necessary to have recourse to contact in order to magnetise him anew. The look of the magnetiser, his volition alone, possess the same influence.
16. In general, changes, more or less remarkable, are produced upon the perception and other mental faculties of those who fall into somnambulism in consequence of magnetism.

(*a*) Some persons amidst the noise of confused conversation hear only the voice of the magnetiser, several answer precisely the questions he puts to them or which are addressed to them by those individuals with whom they have been placed in magnetic connection ; others carry on conversation with all the persons around them.

Nevertheless, it is seldom that they hear what is passing around them. During the greater part of the time they are complete strangers to the external and unexpected noise which is made close to their ears, such as the sound of copper vessels struck briskly near them, the fall of a piece of furniture, etc.

(*b*) The eyes are closed, the eyelids yield with difficulty to the efforts which are made to open them; this operation, which is not without pain, shows the ball of the eye convulsed and carried upwards and sometimes turned towards the lower part of the orbit.

(*c*) Sometimes the power of smelling appears to be annihilated. They may be made to inhale muriatic acid or ammonia without feeling any inconvenience, nay, without perceiving it. The contrary takes place in certain cases, and they retain the sense of smell.

(*d*) The greater number of the somnambulists whom we have seen were completely insensible. We might tickle their feet, their nostrils, and the angle of the eyes with a feather; we might pinch their skin so as to leave a mark, prick them with pins under the nails, etc., without producing any pain, without even their perceiving it. Finally, we saw one who was insensible to one of the most painful operations in surgery, and who did not manifest the slightest emotion in her countenance, her pulse, or her respiration.

17. Magnetism is as intense and as speedily felt at a distance of six feet as of six inches, and the

phenomena developed are the same in both cases.

18. The action at a distance does not appear capable of being executed with success excepting upon individuals who have been already magnetised.
19. We only saw one person who fell into somnambulism upon being magnetised for the first time. Sometimes somnambulism was not manifested until the eighth or tenth sitting.
20. We have invariably seen the ordinary sleep, which is the repose of the organs of sense, of the intellectual faculties, and the voluntary motions, precede and terminate the state of somnambulism.
21. While in the state of somnambulism the patients, whom we have observed, retained the use of the faculties which they possessed when awake. Even their memory appeared to be more faithful and more extensive, because they remembered everything that passed at the time and every time they were placed in the state of somnambulism.
22. Upon awaking they said they had totally forgotten the circumstances which took place during the somnambulism and never recollected them. For this fact we can have no other authority than their own declarations.
23. The muscular powers of somnambulists are

sometimes benumbed and paralysed. At other times their motions are constrained, and the somnambulists walk or totter about like drunken men, sometimes avoiding and sometimes not avoiding the obstacles which may happen to be in their way. There are some somnambulists who preserve entire the power of motion; there are even some who display more strength and agility than in their waking state.

24. We have seen two somnambulists who distinguished, with their eyes closed, the objects which were placed before them; they mentioned the colour and the value of cards without touching them; they read words traced with the hand, as also some lines of books opened at random. The phenomena took place even when the eyes were kept tightly closed with the fingers.

25. In two somnambulists we found the faculty of foreseeing the acts of the organism more or less remote, more or less complicated. One of them announced repeatedly, several months previously, the day, the hour, and the minute of the access and return of epileptic fits. The other announced the period of his cure. Their previsions were realised with remarkable exactness. They appeared to us to apply only to acts or injuries of their organism.

26. We found only a single somnambulist who

pointed out the symptoms of the diseases of three persons with whom she was placed in magnetic connection. We had, however, made experiments upon a considerable number.

27. In order to establish with any degree of exactness the connection between magnetism and therapeutics, it would be necessary to have observed its effects upon a great number of individuals and to have made experiments every day, for a long time, upon the same patients. As this did not take place with us, your committee could only mention what they perceived in too small a number of cases to enable them to pronounce any judgment.

28. Some of the magnetised patients felt no benefit from the treatment. Others experienced a more or less decided relief — viz., one, the suspension of habitual pains; another, the return of his strength; a third, the retardation for several months of his epileptic fits; and a fourth, the complete cure of a serious paralysis of long standing.

29. Considered as a cause of certain physiological phenomena, or as a therapeutic remedy, magnetism ought to be allowed a place within the circle of the medical sciences, and consequently, physicians only should practise it, or superintend its use, as is the case in the northern countries.

30. Your committee have not been able to verify, because they had no opportunity of doing so, other faculties which the magnetiser had announced as existing in somnambulists. But they have communicated in their report facts of sufficient importance to entitle them to think that the Academy ought to encourage the investigations into the subject of animal magnetism as a very curious branch of psychology and natural history.

> (Signed) BOURDOIS DE LA MOTTE, *President;* FOUQUIER, GUENEAU DE MUSSY, GUERSENT, HUSSON, ITARD, J. J. LEROUX, MARC, THILLAYE.
>
> "*Note.*—MM. DOUBLE and MAGENDIE did not consider themselves entitled to sign the report as they had not assisted in making the experiments."

As long as the theory of hypnotic suggestion remained unknown, it was impossible for any investigator to avoid falling into many errors. The reader will notice in the report itself the result of this ignorance; but as a critical and scientific examination of the states, so far as the then existing knowledge allowed, the report cannot be too highly praised. The fact that in the investigation of a subject so surrounded with pitfalls, they drew so few erroneous conclusions testifies, more than anything else, to the thoroughness of their work.

The Academy, however, seemed to be dumbfounded at the impudence of the Commission, and could hardly reconcile itself to believing that their own selected committee had dared to report in favour of magnetism.

History repeats itself sometimes in amusing ways. Recently the British Medical Association nominated a learned committee to investigate and report on "Hypnotism," and on the committee bringing in their report, it was referred back to them as "seeming to bind the medical profession to the use of hypnotism"![1] The mistakes which the French commission made were mainly due to the element of suggestion not being satisfactorily eliminated, though in addition to this primary error they bestowed an amount of attention on the extra-normal phenomena, such as those presented by hysterical patients, not at all proportionate to the results obtained. The importance given to this more or less mystical side of the question provided the Academy with a much desired excuse for ignoring the report as far as possible.

Thus, this second investigation, so far from setting at rest any of the disputed points, only served to

---

[1] At the Annual General Meeting on Aug. 1, 1893, when this report, with amplifications, was again presented, it was *received*—*i.e.*, neither adopted nor rejected.

intensify the general doubt and wonder. The controversy became more keen, the recriminations more violent, as time went on, and in 1837 a fresh attempt was made to arrive at some definite conclusion on the subject. One, by name Berna, urged the Academy to grant another commission to examine his experiments, and a committee was appointed in answer to his continued requests. Their report was published on July 17, 1837, and they made a *résumé* of their researches in the seven conclusions which follow.

First Conclusion.

It results from all the facts and incidents which we have witnessed that, first of all, no special proof has been given us of the existence of a special state called the state of *magnetic somnambulism;* that it is solely by *assertion* not proof that the magnetiser has proceeded in this respect, by affirming to us at each seance and before any attempt at experiment, that his subjects were in a state of somnambulism.

The programme given us by the operator stated, it is true, that the subject enjoyed his full sensibility, in proof of which he could be pricked, and would afterwards be sent to sleep in presence of the committee. But it results from the experiments we made at the seance of the 3rd March, and before any magnetic process, that the subject did not seem to feel the pricking before the supposed sleep more than during it, that his bearing and answers were much the same before and during the operation called magnetic. Was it a mistake on his part? Was it natural impassibility or one acquired by habit? Was it to at once make himself interesting? That is what the committee are unable to decide. It is true afterwards that each time we have been told that the subjects were asleep; but we were *told*, and nothing more.

And if the proofs of the somnambulistic state were later on to result from experiments on subjects supposed to be in that state, the valuelessness and worthlessness of these proofs would follow from the conclusions we are about to draw from these very experiments.

Second Conclusion.

According to the programme, the second seance was to consist in testing the insensibility of the subjects. But, after recalling the restrictions imposed on your committee, that the face was excluded from any such experiment; that the same was the case for all parts naturally covered, so that the hands and neck alone remained: after recalling that, on these parts were allowed neither pinching or pulling, nor contact with a body either ignited or at a somewhat high temperature; that we had to confine ourselves to inserting needles to a depth of about half a line;[1] and lastly that the face being partly covered by a bandage, we could not judge of the expression of the face whilst trying to cause pain; after recalling all these restrictions, we are justified in deducing—1st, that only *very slight and limited* painful sensations could be produced; 2nd, and that, only on a few parts perhaps used to this kind of impressions; 3rd, that this kind of impression was always the same, that it resulted from a kind of *tatooing;* 4th, that the face and especially the eyes, where painful expressions most easily show themselves, were hidden from the committee; that owing to these circumstances even absolute, complete impassibility could not have been to us a conclusive proof of the abolition of sensibility in the aforesaid subject.

Third Conclusion.

The magnetiser was to prove to the committee that by his mere will he could restore, either locally or generally, sensibility to his subject: this he called *restitution* of sensibility.

But as it had been impossible for him to prove to us by experiments that he had removed or abolished sensibility in this young lady, this experiment being correlative to the last, it has been for that very

---

[1] *I.e.*, about $\frac{1}{24}$th of an inch.

reason impossible to prove this restitution; and besides it results from the facts we have observed, that all essays in this direction have failed. The subject described quite the reverse of what he had announced. You remember, gentlemen, that we were reduced for verification to the assertion of the subject; when she affirmed for instance that she could not move her left leg, that surely was no proof to the committee that she was magnetically paralysed in that member; but even then her words disagreed with the pretensions of the magnetiser; so that from all this resulted assertions without proof, opposed to other assertions equally without proof.

Fourth Conclusion.

What we have just said about the abolition and restitution of sensibility, applies to the pretended abolition and restitution of movement; not the slightest proof could be given to the committee.

Fifth Conclusion.

One of the sections of the programme was entitled: "*Obedience to a mental order to cease, in the middle of a conversation, and to answer verbally or by signs a particular person.*"

The magnetiser tried, in the seance of March 13th, to prove to the committee that the power of his will could produce this effect; but it results from what took place, that far from producing these results, the subject seemed to no longer hear before he wanted to prevent her from so doing, and that she again seemed to hear when he positively did not want her to hear; so that, from the subject's assertions, the faculty of hearing or not hearing would have been, in her, in complete opposition to the will of the magnetiser.

But, after well understood facts, the committee no more conclude an opposition them a submission; they have found a complete independence and nothing more.

SIXTH CONCLUSION.

Transposition of Sight.

Yielding to the entreaty of the committee, the magnetiser, as we have seen, had left alone his abolitions and restitutions of sensibility and movement to come to the more important facts—viz., vision without the use of the eyes. All the incidents relative to this have been told you; they took place at the seance of 3rd April 1837.

By the power of his magnetic passes, M. Berna was to show the committee a woman reading words, recognising playing-cards, following the hands of a watch, not with the eyes but with the occiput, which implied either the transposition, or the uselessness, or the superfluity of the organ of sight in the magnetic state. The experiments took place; you know how they utterly failed.

All that the subject knew, all she could infer from what was said near her, all she could naturally suppose, she told while she was blindfolded; from which we conclude, first of all, that she did not lack a certain amount of skill. Thus the magnetiser invited one of the committee to write a word on a card and present it to this woman's occiput; she said she could see a card and even some writing on it. Were she asked the number of people present, since she had seen them enter, she said approximately the number of persons. Were she asked whether she saw a certain member of the committee placed near her, writing with a squeaky pen, she would raise her head, try to see under the bandage, and said the person held something white in his hand. Asked whether she could say what was in the mouth of this person who, ceasing to write, had placed himself behind her, she would say he had something white in his mouth; from which we conclude that the said subject was more experienced and skilled than the first, and knew how to make more plausible suppositions. But, as for facts really fit to prove sight by the occiput, decisive, absolute unanswerable facts, not only were they wanting, entirely wanting, but those we saw were of such a nature as to make us conceive strange suspicions as to the morality of this woman, as we will presently show.

Seventh Conclusion.

Giving up the hope of proving to the committee the transposition of sight, the uselessness of the eyes in the magnetic state, the magnetiser wished to take refuge in clairvoyance or sight through opaque bodies.

You know the experiments made on this point; here facts carry with them their chief conclusion, viz., that a man placed before a woman in a certain position was unable to make her distinguish, through a bandage, objects presented to her.

But here a more grave thought occupied the committee. Let us admit for a moment the hypotheses so handy for magnetisers, that at times the best subjects lose all lucidity, and that, like the rest of mortals, they can no longer see by the occiput, stomach, not even across a bandage; let us, if you will, admit all this; but what are we to conclude, with regard to this woman, from her minute description of objects *other* than those presented to her? What can we conclude of a subject who describes a knave of clubs on a blank card, who on a counter sees a gold watch with white dial and black letters, and who, had we insisted, would, perhaps have ended by telling us the time indicated by this watch?

If now, gentlemen, you ask us what last and general conclusion we are to draw from the whole of these experiments made before us, we will say that

M. Berna has, without doubt, deceived himself, when on February 12th of this year, he wrote to the Royal Academy of Medicine that he would undertake to give us the personal experience we lacked (those were his words), when he offered to show your committee *conclusive* facts; when he affirmed these facts would be of a nature to enlighten physiology and therapeutics. You know these facts; you know they are far from conclusive, that they have shown nothing in favour with this doctrine of animal magnetism, that it can have nothing in common with either physiology or therapeutics.

Should we have found anything else in more numerous, more varied cases provided by other magnetisers? We will not attempt to decide; but what is well established is that if other magnetisers still exist, they have not dared to show themselves in daylight, they have not dared to challenge the academical sanction or condemnation.

(Signed) ROUX, *President;* BOUILLAUD, CLOQUET, EMERY, PELLETIER, CAVENTOU, CORNAC, OUDET.

DUBOIS (d'Amiens), reporter.

PARIS, 17*th July* 1837.

It will be seen that in this case the committee reported strongly against Animal Magnetism, and their report was accepted, despite the earnest protests of Husson, by a large majority of the Academy. If the report of 1831 were unsatisfactory and indefinite, this last was even more so. By far the greater part of, if not all, the attention of the commission was devoted to a demonstration of the non-existence of certain alleged magnetic conditions, transposition of the senses, prevision, clairvoyance, etc., etc.

Animal Magnetism itself was but incidentally touched upon. In fact, the commission and the Academy had both been following the wrong scent, and it was regarded as a final settlement when Burdin (the younger), with the approval of the Academy, offered a prize of 3000 francs to any one who could read, or who could produce a person capable of reading, a given writing without the aid of his eyes and in the dark. The first candidate for this prize was a Dr Pigeaire who claimed that his daughter, a young girl about ten years old, could in the somnambulistic state, amongst many other wonders, read writing with her eyes covered by a bandage. He came to Paris, not without credentials. The Professor of Physiology at Montpellier testified to the power possessed by this girl, and in Paris he gave some *séances* before several doctors, who also stated that they had witnessed an exhibition of these powers. In the beginning of the Academy's investigation an hitch occurred with regard to the bandage. The committee would not accept the black silk one provided by Pigeaire. They justly demanded that the bandage should be of such a kind that the subject could neither see over, nor under, nor through it. Under ordinary circumstances, a bandage is but a slight security against fraud, whilst, in the case of a somnambulistic subject, any such provision would be of little value.

Those conducting the investigation, therefore, proposed a light and easy fitting mask, that the vision might be absolutely obscured. To this Pigeaire would not listen, nor would he assent to any modifications proposed by the committee, and, as neither side would agree to the terms proposed by the other, the trial never took place.

One, by name Teste, came before the Academy with greater pretensions and ones that were easily decided. This gentleman produced a somnambulist who, he said, could read a letter or other matter enclosed in a box. The conditions were, in this case, soon agreed upon, and the supposed power as soon shown to be fictitious. The subject was not able to read a word.

Others came forward with similar claims, and, on their failure, complained that the presence of the commissioners had an exciting and disturbing influence on their subjects. The Academicians then said they were ready to award the prize if the contents of the box were divined out of their presence. M. Burdin kept his francs.

That this effectively settled the question of the

super-normal states, with regard to clairvoyance, is apparent, but it by no means decided the controversy with regard to animal magnetism proper. Nevertheless the Academy resolved, chiefly in consequence of these last experiments, that henceforth any propositions of the magnetists should not be entertained, and that the question of magnetism itself should be regarded as definitely and finally closed. This last conclusion can only be described as silly.

The repeated failures of the various commissions, which were composed of the most learned and scientific men of the day, to separate the true from the false, or even to arrive at any near approximation of the truth, affords a striking illustration of the general uselessness of resorting to such means. Every trouble was taken, the most minute investigations, for the greater part of a century were made, and at the end no one was much the wiser than he was at the beginning. The real issues were, throughout, little understood. The magnetisers devoted all their efforts to proving, not the existence of the magnetic state, but phenomena which were only incidental and of real use only to the psychologist; whilst the commissions allowed themselves to be led into the discussion of multitudinous theories to the almost entire neglect of the real question they had been appointed to investigate.

It is given to few to discover, and their discovery is often due to the happy combination of chance and skill. The discovery made, the body, whom it most closely interests, proceeds first to sneer, then to pay a constrained attention, and finally, after having indulged in every species of abuse and vituperation known to man, it yields to the inevitable and recognises the truth.[1]

From about 1825 we hear little of animal magnetism in Germany, though, scattered about the country, there were many thoughtful and critical enquirers. One of the most curious points is its influence on the philosophy of the time. Schopenhauer, and some other less known writers, made magnetism and its phenomena the basis of a large part of their philosophy. In most countries, and in France particularly, the abuses of magnetism common to its vulgar use were increasing year by year. Impostors and charlatans made free use of it for the purposes of extortion and fraud of every kind, whilst the most extravagant and preposterous notions were spreading amongst the ignorant and the credulous concerning it.

There are several instances on record where the clergy practised magnetism with no less an object than that of obtaining supernatural revelations.

[1] Those readers who think this an exaggerated view may find its unhappy confirmation by a reference to the history of the receptions accorded to Harvey's doctrine of the circulation of the blood, Simpson's discovery of chloroform, Jenner's introduction of vaccination, and some other of the great discoveries.

Père Lacordaire preached a sermon in 1846 at Nôtre Dame, eulogising magnetism as a power that would once and for all confound the infidels, and demonstrate to humanity the power of the Infinite.

The Church was constantly intervening in the attempt to check these strange abuses, and in 1856 an encyclical letter was sent to all the bishops "contra abusus magnetismi." It will be found in full at the end of this chapter.

England was late in adopting magnetism. In 1837, however, the amiable but unscientific enthusiast, Du Potet, came to London, where he met Dr John Elliotson of the University College Hospital. Du Potet succeeded in engrafting on his newly-made friend all the magnetic theories, and from this time Elliotson made use of magnetism in the hospital, and adopted it into his regular practice. The council of University College, however, soon passed a resolution against its use in the hospital, and Elliotson at once resigned. The medical papers of the time are curious evidence of what bigotry and ignorance are capable. The most vile and indecent insinuations were levelled at Elliotson, who was, at any rate, a physician of high attainments, and a perfect gentleman. Many of the charges and much of the prejudice, it is only fair to say, were due to the nonsense which Elliotson combined with his mesmeric theories.

The wise man introducing such a novel method of treatment would have been most careful to avoid anything like quackery. Elliotson's experiments became little more than sober fooling. "Clairvoyance" and "Phrenology" were his constant stock-in-trade, whilst he regularly employed the two sisters "Okey" in his operations. No doubt his character was unimpeachable, but he has himself to thank for much of the persecution from which he suffered. Elliotson certainly could only have retarded the progress of hypnotism, and however we may regret the treatment to which he was subjected, it is a matter of congratulation to have been so soon delivered from what Dr Lloyd Tuckey has well called "a mass of superincumbent rubbish."

We now pass from the history of Magnetism to the beginnings of Hypnotism. Dr James Braid of Manchester, instead of contenting himself with the mesmeric theories, placed the subject, for the first time, on a scientific basis, by a careful examination of the phenomena. The Abbé Faria had anticipated his discovery to a certain extent, but he lacked method, and his language was vague and unscientific. Braid entered upon his investigation a complete sceptic. In 1841 he attended a demonstration, given in Manchester by La Fontaine, a magnetist from Switzerland, with the avowed object of endeavouring to discover the means by which the tricks (as he regarded them) were performed. Soon, however, he had to admit that whatever was their explanation, the facts themselves were undeniable; but, unlike Elliotson, he did not rest content with the operator's explanation that the means of the influence was a magnetic fluid, and he set himself to a serious study of the question. The first phenomenon that appears to have attracted his attention, as a possible clue to the secret, was the fact that the subjects were unable to open their eyes. He attributed this to the exhaustion of the optic nerves, and was led thereby to the conclusion, which he verified by experiments, that the induction of hypnosis was due to physiological modifications of the nervous system. Braid tired the nerves of his patients by fixing their gaze on some given object, a method which is very common to-day. He found that it was necessary for the subject to concentrate his thought as well as his vision, or in other words that " expectant attention " was a necessary factor.

Braid primarily demonstrated two things—

1. That the assumption of any such force as a magnetic fluid, mesmeric influence, or other unknown agency, was unnecessary.
2. That the state was a super-normal physiological one induced by a physical or appreciable action on the nervous system.

In order to distinguish these conclusions from the inchoate mass of speculation and superstition known under the name of animal magnetism, he invented the term "*Hypnotism.*"

Braid has left accounts of his various experiments and observations which show the thoroughness of his examinations, whilst they are also important as evidence of the development of the science since his time. He found that verbal suggestion was sufficient to produce hallucination, and this was a contribution to the subject of the highest importance; but he had not fathomed the theory of suggestion, and this was left for later writers, first and foremost Dr Liébault of Nancy, to examine more fully.

The attitude would, Braid observed, affect the sentiments of the subject. With his fists clenched, the subject would assume an angry expression and prepare to fight; a pleasing action would promote a corresponding mental mood. Then again, in his *Neurypnology* he details a series of experiments in "phreno-hypnotism." By pressing on the phrenological "organs" he found he could induce the emotions belonging to each; thus, by pressing on the "organ of veneration," the subject would kneel in the attitude of prayer; if the "organ of acquisitiveness" were touched, the subject would steal, and so forth. Phrenology has been exploded till it is beneath explosion; yet these subjects were unquestionably honest and genuine. The source of his error lay in his failure to recognise that the hypnotised subject is extremely sensitive to suggestion: a word, a gesture, a remark of one of the spectators, is often sufficient to indicate the wish of the operator. To this feature of *unconscious suggestion* are due nearly all the fallacies of serious students of hypnotism.

It is also a curious fact that, in most cases of deep hypnosis, the subject, when hypnotised, remembers the events which took place on the previous hypnoses, though he knows nothing of them in the waking state. It is thus frequently possible, by an uniform adherence to certain touches for certain actions or emotions, for the hypnotist to dispense altogether with verbal suggestion, and rely on the touch, which the subject will instantly interpret in the desired manner. Braid was remarkably successful in the application of hypnotism to the alleviation and cure of disease, and it is difficult to explain how, after his death, the subject came to be practically forgotten. Carpenter, the great physiologist, supported him, and others of high repute. It has been thought probable that Elliotson's experience frightened Braid from attempting to at all hastily force his ideas on the profession; but he, in fact, was indefatigable in its advocacy and cannot be accused of undue caution.

The fact seems to be, that just about this time chloroform was introduced, and those of the medical profession who had paid any serious attention to hypnotism persisted in placing its chief value in the anæsthetic properties of deep hypnosis. No hypnotist would maintain that hypnotism could ever be used as an universal anæsthetic, though it may be of the greatest value in cases where the administration of the usual anæsthetics would be dangerous or inexpedient.

This point, however, was quite neglected, and on the use of chloroform coming in, hypnotism seems to have been ignored, only to be reintroduced into England within quite recent years. Littré and Robin, and others, published extracts from Braid's writings in France, and Meunier wrote an article for the *Présse;* but the interest was for some time purely theoretical and Braid's discovery attracted little attention. However, in 1850, Azam, a surgeon of Bordeaux, tried experiments, suggested by Braid's writings, on a patient suffering from spontaneous catalepsy. He also made experiments on another patient, and found they confirmed Braid's conclusions. He published the results in the *Archives de Médecine.* In France, too, the endeavour was made to use hypnotism as a general anæsthetic; the difficulty was increased since it was not known that insensibility could be produced by suggestion, and thus only the subjects in the deepest forms of hypnosis could be operated on without pain. Its use for such purposes was soon rejected in favour of chloroform. From 1860, many competent investigators were engaged on the subject, and a number of works were published dealing with the subject. In 1866 appeared the famous work by Dr Liébault, entitled "Du Sommeil et des États Analogues," etc. At the time of its publication, however, it was received with much derision by the medical faculty, but within recent years a change has come over the scene, and Liébault is quoted and referred to largely by every writer on hypnotism or kindred subjects. For a long time Liébault laboured at Nancy, but little noticed by his profession. In 1882, M. Dumont, who had witnessed the methods and practice in vogue at Nancy, tried some experiments on his own account. The results were so successful that he read a paper to the Medical Society thoroughly supporting Liébault's methods and treatment. This combined, possibly, with Charcot's experiments at Salpêtrière, led Dr Bernheim to investigate the subject. He, by his own account, set to work in a very sceptical spirit, but met with results so striking and certain that he felt bound to speak. Bernheim already possessed a wide reputation, and his adoption of hypnotism had at once the effect of securing for the subject a much more patient hearing than had ever before been the case.

Many scientists in France and Germany had interested themselves in hypnotism, but it was not till the school of Nancy dealt with the question that it took up a real position in the science of medicine. Bernheim, who had devoted himself to its study with Liébault, published his work "De la

Suggestion," etc., in 1884. Nancy became the headquarters of the leading French hypnotists. There Beaunis and Liégois worked at the physiological and the medico-legal aspects of the question. The contests between the schools of the Salpêtrière and Nancy soon followed, and every year has served to increase the reputation, amongst scientists of all nations, of Liébault and his followers, whilst Charcot's school, despite the leader's eminence in his own branch, has become more and more discredited till, outside Paris, their views are hardly represented at all.

To enumerate the many students and writers in the various countries, would be a lengthy task. It must suffice to say, that, besides the two countries France and Germany, Russia, Denmark, Norway, Sweden, Greece, Italy, Spain, Switzerland, Belgium, Austria, the United States, South America are all represented by many patient and learned investigators; whilst in England Dr Milne Bramwell of Goole, Dr Kingsbury of Blackpool, and especially Dr Lloyd Tuckey of London, have contributed work of the highest order. The British Medical Association has found hypnotism "worthy of investigation," though, apparently, it could hardly reconcile itself quite so suddenly to the course recommended by the committee they appointed to investigate and report on the question.[1]

Mention must be made of a few who hold many

[1] *Vide* note on p. 51.

of the mesmeric ideas. The Society for Psychical Research is responsible for most of them in England. The work done by Myers and Gurney, under its auspices, must rank high, and they have provided much that claims our attention and investigation. Edmund Gurney died some time ago, but the work has been carried on by Myers and others. Though this Society has published some valuable records of its work in this direction, they can hardly be considered convincing, having regard to all the circumstances; and, indeed, they have not yet claimed that their experiments can be considered as at all conclusive.

For those who may be curious as to the "morality" of hypnotism, I append two quotations; the first shows the view taken by the Church in 1856, and will probably appeal only to Catholics; the sound common-sense of the second, which is quoted from a theologian of the Society of Jesus, will, I think, be appreciated by all.

The Roman decree runs as follows :—[1]

"At the general congregation of the Holy Roman Inquisition held in the convent Sancta Maria (above Minerva), the Cardinals, and Inquisitors-general against heresy throughout the Christian world, after a careful examination of all that has been reported to them by trustworthy men, touching the practice of magnetism, have resolved to address

[1] "Epistola Encyclica S. Rom. Inquisitionis ad omnes Episcopos adversus magnetismi abusus." *Vide* Compendium Theologiae Moralis. Gury.

the present encyclical letter to all the bishops in order that its abuses may be repressed. For it is clearly established that a new species of superstition has arisen, with regard to the magnetic phenomena, with which many are now concerned, not with the legitimate object of elucidating the physical sciences, but in order to deceive and mislead men, under the belief that things hidden, remote or in the future, may be revealed by means of magnetism, and especially by the aid of certain women who are completely under the magnetist's control.

"The Holy See, when consulted in particular cases, has repeatedly replied by condemning as unlawful all experiments made to obtain a result opposed to the natural order and to the moral law, and to obtain which unlawful means are made use of. It was in such cases that it was decided on the 21st of April 1841, that magnetism as set forth in this petition is not permissible. So, likewise, the holy congregation deemed it well to forbid the use of certain books which systematically diffuse error on this subject. But since, exclusive of special cases, it became necessary to pronounce on the practice of magnetism in general, the following rule was established on July 18, 1847 :—'All error being removed, sorcery, the invocation of spirits, explicit or implicit, the use of magnetism, that is, the simple act of employing physical means, not otherwise forbidden, is not morally illegal so long as it is for no illicit or evil object.

"'But the application of purely physical principles and means to things or results which are in reality supernatural, so as to give them a physical explanation, is nothing but a delusion, and is altogether illegal and heretical.'

"Although this decree sufficiently explains what is lawful or unlawful in the use or abuse of magnetism, human perversity is such that men who have devoted themselves to the discovery of whatever ministers to curiosity, greatly to the detriment of the salvation of souls, and even to that of civil society, boast that they have found the means of prediction and divination. Hence it follows that weak-minded women, thrown by gestures, which are not always modest, into a state of somnambulism, and of what is called *clairvoyance*, profess to see those things which are invisible, and claim with rash audacity the power of speaking on religious matters, of calling up the spirits of the dead, of receiving answers to their enquiries, and of discovering what is unknown or remote. They practise other superstitions of like nature, in order that, by this gift of divination, they may procure considerable gain for themselves and their masters. Whatever be the arts or illusions employed in these acts, since physical means are used to obtain unnatural results, the imposture is worthy of condemnation, since it is heretical and a scandal against the purity of morals. In order, therefore, effectually to repress so great an evil, which is most fatal to religion and to civil society, the pastoral care, vigilance, and zeal of all the bishops cannot be too earnestly invoked. Aided by divine grace, the ordinary of each diocese must do all in his power, both by the admonitions of paternal love, by severe reproaches, and, finally, by legal means, using these according to his judgment before the Lord, and taking account of the circumstances, of place, of time, and persons; to avert the abuse of magnetism and to bring it to an end, so that the Lord's flock may be preserved from the attacks of the enemy, that the faith may be maintained in its integrity, and that the faithful committed to their care may be saved from the corruption of morals.

"Given at Rome, at the Chancery of the Sacred Office, at the Vatican.

"V. CARD. MACCHI."

"*4th of August* 1856."

The Catholic Church, it will be noticed from the quotation above, drew a very strong distinction between the use of magnetism for any natural purpose and the superstitious use of it for the attainment of some result contrary to the natural order. This distinction was the more necessary at the time when the Encyclical was issued, since the extravagant claims of the mystic magnetists were then being put forward with extraordinary energy and persistence.

As hypnotism is of comparatively recent origin it

has so far received the attention of but few of the casuists. The following extract, however, taken from the latest Moral Theology of the Jesuits, places the moral question on a very clear footing.

The following is the translation of the Latin :—[1]

"In dealing with the superstitions of magnetism, I have necessarily touched on the great question of 'animal magnetism' as it is called, whether, to what extent, and when, it may be allowed as a remedy for the curing of disease. Recently many of those things which were formerly attributed to magnetism are now explained on other grounds, and attributed to that to which the name 'hypnotism' has been given; namely, a wonderful art so that by means of the fixed gaze at one object and the concentration of mind on one thing, a state of mind is produced in which the functions of the nerves and of a certain part of the brain are inhibited; reflex consciousness ceases, the man, under the influence, does all things at the will of another; he manifests, unknowingly, his natural inclinations, and the deeper his sleep, things the more strange he does or suffers. This method is praised as being more reliable in surgical operations, as an anæsthetic, and as one by means of which the diseases of the brain and of the nerves, rheumatism, etc., may be easily cured.

"By the theologian the inquiry has to be made whether this remedy be a legitimate one. It is not

[1] Theologia Moralis. A. Lehmkuhl, S.J.

possible to deny its lawfulness except either—
(1) The mode of inducing the state is unlawful, or
(2) The state itself is unlawful. In the *mode* it does not seem possible to hold that there is anything unlawful, except injury or superstition enter into it. I cannot think injury is done since the subject must consent, and, moreover, it is said that a man can throw himself into the state. Superstition, of itself, does not enter in, if the methods and state remain as I have described. For it is certain that unaccustomed changes take place in a man, by the alteration of the nerves and brain, in an altogether natural manner; it is, moreover, agreed that the most complete hallucinations can be caused by perfectly natural means. Whether, therefore, you consider the state can be induced in a healthy man, or whether you consider it requires, rather, a certain morbid state of the nerves, you always have a natural method of treatment.

" Is the *state* then illicit ?

" You have the deprivation of reason and a state in which you reveal the most private matter, and in which, without consciousness or freedom, you follow the bidding of another. Therefore the more such a state appears unfitting for a man the graver must be the necessary reason by virtue of which it may be allowable to induce such a state; nor will its induction ever be lawful except with the exercise of caution.

"Therefore— 1. It is not lawful without there be a *relatively* serious cause, since you always have a state and method *violent*, and in this state the man is deprived of the use of reason, and that not in an ordinary manner, as in sleep.

"2. It will never be lawful without the exercise of due caution; lest some one should injure the man so sent to sleep, especially as the man cannot rouse himself from the state. Wherefore, except the operator be a trustworthy man, I should refuse to place myself in his hands. But, due caution being observed, and there being a sufficient reason, hypnotism would be lawful, the more so if it be true that diseases otherwise incurable are by this means to be cured; but this ought to be investigated under the sober experience of skilled physicians, and not to be lightly believed since it is well known that such things are often told, which, on being enquired into, are found to be mere delusions."

The Jesuit, in describing the state itself, has certainly overstated the case, for it must be remembered that only a proportion of hypnotised subjects are sufficiently under the influence to manifest their natural inclinations without care or discretion, and, indeed, it is still a matter of controversy as to how far the deepest subjects will prejudice themselves by any act or word of theirs when in the hypnotic state. It is certain that in a large proportion of subjects in the deepest forms of hypnosis a criminal suggestion will not be obeyed, and it has been clearly shown that the success of such a suggestion would depend upon the moral character of the subject.

Fr. Lehmkuhl's argument, however, gains rather than loses any force by reason of these qualifications; it is evident that if the induction of the deepest state, when possible, be contrary to no moral law, there can be no suspicion against the induction of any of the lighter stages.

It may be fairly claimed that hypnotism has now gained a position in the scientific world that makes it imperative on all medical and psychological students to study the facts and properties of hypnotism. The medical man who would frighten his patients by telling them tales of insanity following the induction of hypnosis, and the various fictions with which most are familiar, is beginning to be generally recognised as one using long words and ominous sentences wherewith to cloak his own ignorance. At the same time, it ought to be understood, by all, that the dangers of the unscientific and ignorant use of hypnotism are manifold; and it is to be hoped that, before long, the State will intervene to regulate its use by rendering the practice of hypnotism illegal except in the hands of duly qualified men under proper restrictions.

CHAPTER III.

MENTAL ACTION.

The human mind and the logical faculty—The emotional faculty—The influence of environment—The opposite influence—The necessity of predisposition—The harmony of the reason and emotion—The basis of reason—Unity of impressions—Mental influence on the animal functions—The condition of sleep—The Dacoits—Coma—Examples of sleep allied to coma—The dreaming state—Conditions for the induction of sleep—The receptivity of the sleeping state — The nature of the dreaming state — Somnambulism — Views of Liébault, Bernheim, Moll, and Tuckey on sleep—The analogies of the waking state—Müller—Herbert Spencer—Ideas and sensorial impressions—Examples of these—Ideation—The origination by nerve centres—Suspension of the inhibitory centre—Suggestion—Different forms of this—Automatic and voluntary actions—Increased power due to combined action of these — The intellect and sensations—Braid's experiments—Other illustrations—Dr Wigan—Herbert Spencer—John Hunter—Involuntary actions—The intellect and the organic functions—Hysteria—Religious convulsions—The Fakirs—The Aïssouans—Wesley—Shakerism—Ochorowicz—The subjective nature of hypnosis.

THE hypnotist is frequently asked to give a simple and complete explanation of the phenomena of hypnosis, and such a request is reasonable if it be clearly understood that the explanation must be more or less tentative and in proportion to our knowledge of the normal mental state. It is, however, apt to be forgotten that our knowledge of this normal condition is very limited, and depends altogether on the observation of its phenomena;

of the actual nature of the mental processes we are entirely ignorant. Any attempt, therefore, to propound a theory which should absolutely elucidate the mental state produced in hypnosis would be plainly fruitless, and we must be content, in the investigation of this abnormal condition, to proceed on exactly the same lines which have been followed in the case of the normal and common conditions of the brain. Our object, then, is a comparison of results ; we take, first, the phenomena of the brain in its various states outside hypnosis, and compare them with the hypnotic phenomena; so that we may arrive with a fair degree of certainty at the essential points of difference between the two conditions

It is necessary to predicate of the human mind—

1. That the logical faculty of the brain is chiefly the result of training and education.
2. That this logical faculty, even in the spheres where it should be most used, is always modified by the senses of emotion and affection ; whilst, in the predisposition towards certain modes of thought and action, heredity plays an important part.

The exercise of discrimination in the acceptance of statement and dogma comes to us as we recognise the necessity of such scepticism. During childhood this faculty does not exist, and statement and dogma are impressed on the infant mind without arousing any logical resistance; nor does the child possess any reasoning consciousness of possible error. Thus the education of the child, unless it be peculiarly and exceptionally wise, tends to restrain the action of free-will, and it may be doubted whether any mind is capable of altogether withdrawing itself from the bonds of training, circumstance, and environment, to which during its infancy it has been subjected. For the mind of great reflective and analytical power is apt to resent all ideas which appear to have been impressed on it by such means, and is, in consequence, attracted by views and theories of an opposite nature. Thus, in the latter case, there is a prejudice against belief, and, in the former, there is a wish to believe; both impulses springing not from an inherent power in the mind but from an external impression.

Nor do men base their reasonable acts on any logical process; the object of the public speaker, of the religious preacher, of any one who tries, with any success, to bring the majority round to his side, is not to put before his hearers or readers a course of philosophic thought in which no flaw is to be found, but, rather, to touch some common chord, and elicit for his doctrines a sympathetic predisposition and attention. Given this, his views do not meet with the calculating, fault-finding criticism of the cold opponent, but are received by minds already prepared to explain away difficulties and invent further theories of their own to account for any apparent inconsistency or want of harmony.

It may be said, however, that these are common errors referred to in every primer of logic, and that they have only to be seen and understood to be avoided. Yet the very avoidance of these errors is apt to lead to a not uncommon fault; a certain frigid exclusiveness of mind which despises all popular effort, and views with contempt every movement of the majority to put things on a sounder basis; so that, whatever be the disposition of the mind, it is never really governed by the laws of pure reason. In the belief of a proposition it is actuated by the desire to believe, whilst, in the opposite case, it is moved by the wish not to believe; or, in other words, emotion and not logic is the basis of our reasonable actions.

Thus logic provides excuses and smooths the way for, but does not primarily induce, the acceptance or rejection of any dogma.

Nevertheless, the very use of the logical faculty to justify a course of action, primarily instituted by the emotion, is an evidence of the importance given to reason; and, as the critical side of the mind is more cultivated, so will the emotional become more modified, the result being an intellectual harmony hard to realise and incapable of analysis.

Still, however subdued or modified this emotional part of the brain may be, it is never altogether absent, and indeed, if not in all, at least in the majority, it may be said to predominate.

The real and proper use of the logical faculty is plainly the pursuit of knowledge—a pursuit dictated by the love of truth. Thus not only is the belief or the disbelief of any proposition an act in which the logical and the emotional are combined, but the cause of such intellectual action is purely emotional.

That these statements may seem rash and paradoxical is more than probable; yet it is only possible to avoid these conclusions if we are able to show that there are any whose acts and thoughts, in their origin and execution, are purely logical. We have, therefore, a mental state to consider which, in its normal condition, is the result of an elaborate balancing of ideas, sentiments, theories, and facts; neither the reason nor the emotion are capable of acting entirely independently of one another, but perform their functions in such subtle harmony that no single act can be described as purely reasonable, emotional, or ideational. It follows, then, that an impression made on the emotional centre of the brain by no means remains merely an emotional impression, but will lead the reasoning faculty to adapt the actions it dictates, to an harmony with the emotions aroused; and so it is with all the centres of the brain; an impression is not confined to the particular centre which is primarily affected, but extends its influence over the whole brain.

As we study the phenomena of what is termed suggestion, we see the importance of clearly appreciating this complex action of the brain, in virtue of which an impression received by a single sense is converted, by the persistent tendency of the brain to harmonise all its perceptions and emotions, into an impression received and endorsed by the whole of the reasoning and perceptive faculties.

But thus far we have only touched on the psychological aspect of this mental action; we have still to note that, if the brain be the organ of the mind, it is equally the organ of the animal functions.

To its initiative is due every act of the body, and here again the harmony of the human organism is even more apparent. Illness of the body will result in illness of the mind. We have only to stay in a town where the climate is enervating to find that a corresponding lassitude of mind accompanies the enfeebling of the animal functions.

Again, we feel ill and go to the theatre or spend some time amidst a brilliant society and forget, in the excitement and pleasure of the moment, our ills and pains, to find, when we cease from the enjoyment, that we no longer feel ill and depressed but well and happy.

And every reader will be able to find from his own experience many examples of this correspondence between the mind and the body.

The degree of influence which is exerted over the body by the mind necessarily varies largely; in the person of dull, heavy, and stupid disposition its results are by no means striking; to the brilliant, vivacious disposition, where the mental instrument is of fine adjustment and delicate structure, we look for our best examples; whilst we learn much from the study of those abnormal cases, where the brain is over sensitive and more or less out of balance, and where, in consequence, results are obtained of a strange and wonderful character.

We have, then, to consider the various states of the brain in the many aspects it presents under normal and under exceptional conditions.

Firstly, we will consider very briefly and cursorily the state of normal sleep.

Profound sleep is a suspension of the animal powers of sense and motion. In this state the consciousness is not excited by the transmission of sensation to the brain, nor by the transmission from the brain of nervous impulses. During the deepest sleep the animal processes proceed uninterruptedly. Pulsation, respiration, continue; while the unconsciousness of the sleeper remains apparently perfect he is capable of adapting himself to outside circumstances; thus, he will turn in his bed from weariness of the same posture; will rub a limb or any part of his body in order to allay irritation. Carpenter, whose study of sleep in his "Mental Physiology" I am following, quotes a case showing the possible adaptation of actions to a definite purpose. "It is said that the Dacoits or professional thieves of India have been known to steal a mattress from beneath a sleeper, by taking advantage of this tendency. They begin by intensifying his sleep, by gently fanning his face, and then, when they judge him to be in a state of profound insensibility, they gently tickle whatever part of his body may lie most conveniently for their purpose. The sleeper withdrawing himself from this irritation towards the edge of the mattress, the thief again fans his face for a while, and repeats the tickling which causes a further movement. And at last the sleeper edges himself off the mattress, with which the thief makes away."

Profound sleep is to be distinguished from *coma* by the fact that, in the one case, it can be ended by strong sense-impressions, whilst, in the other, the sleeper cannot be aroused; but there are transitional stages between the two. Sleep may partake of the nature of *coma*.

During the heat of the battle of the Nile some of the powder boys fell asleep upon the deck: and during the attack upon Rangoon, in the early Burmese war, the captain of one of the steam-frigates most actively engaged, worn out by the continued mental tension, fell asleep, and remained perfectly unconscious for two hours, within a yard of one of his largest guns which was being worked energetically during the whole period.

Between the condition of normal profound sleep and the normal waking state, there are many gradations.

The *dreaming* state seems to be one in which that part of the brain, receiving the nervous impulses of external sensation, is fully contracted by reason of the withdrawal of the proper blood supply from the brain; whilst the centre for the internal impulses of the cerebrum is only partially contracted, and, in consequence, the brain is conscious of intellectual sensation, but is unconscious of any external sense impression.

For the induction of sleep several concomitant conditions are necessary.

1. An exhaustion of potential energy in the brain cells, caused by previous functional activity.
2. A less and decreasing flow of blood through the brain.
3. Chemical changes in the tissue and brain due to the waste products caused by nervous action.

There are other conditions more or less necessary, such as a comfortable posture, a peaceful state of the mind, the absence of external excitement, etc.

Sometimes, however, the presence of external

excitement is necessary; those accustomed to sleep in the midst of great noise find it difficult to sleep when there is perfect silence.

Monotonous repetitions have a tendency to induce sleep; the unvarying accents of an unskilful preacher are an instance.

The transition from the waking to the sleeping state, and *vice versa*, may be sudden; but generally there is a noticeable gradation. Thus, the man who, when sitting in his arm-chair, "dozes" is brought back to a partial degree of consciousness by his head falling forward. It is a common experience with many to wake up at any time they may have previously decided upon. This is a fact of peculiar importance, and indeed, the very familiarity with many strange facts prevents our proper appreciation of them. It is possible to awake an heavy sleeper by means which would fail entirely with another—the means being incident to his calling or profession. Dr Carpenter gives a graphic illustration of this:—

"Most sleepers are awoke by the sound of *their own names* uttered in a low tone; when it requires a much louder sound of a different description to produce any manifestation of consciousness. The same thing is seen in comatose states; a patient being often found capable of being momentarily aroused by shouting his name into his ear, when no other sound produces the least effect. The medical practitioner, in his first profound sleep after a laborious day, is awoke by the first stroke of the clapper of his night-bell, or even by the movement of the bell-wire which precedes it. The telegraph-clerk, however deep the repose in which he has lost the remembrance of his previous vigils, is recalled to activity by the faintest sound produced by the vibration of the signalling needle, to whose indications he is required to give diligent heed. The mother, whose anxiety for her offspring is for a time the dominant feeling in her mind, is aroused from the refreshing slumber in which all her cares have been forgotten, by the slightest wail of uneasiness proceeding from her infant charge."

Thus, in ordinary sleep there is often present a peculiar *receptivity* for certain definite sense-impressions acquired by reason of the previous direction of the mind.

Dreaming sleep presents many noteworthy peculiarities. The consciousness of the external is completely absent; the mind is more or less active; consciousness of this action is more or less present, and the subsequent remembrance of the dream is sometimes complete, sometimes hazy, and sometimes non-existent.

All control over the current of thought is suspended. There are many instances where the sleeper in his dream has been able to complete calculations, write poems, compose music. The present writer has twice solved problems in the dreaming state, and has remembered sufficient of the train of thought, on waking, to be able to put the solutions down on paper. These, however, are exceptional; and by far the most common dream is that in which the thoughts run on, from one circumstance to another, in an incongruous and ridiculous maze.

Here we have a striking resemblance to the hypnotic state. In the dream the ridiculously impossible chain of events excites neither wonder nor surprise. There is no operator to suggest a train of thought or an idea, and the active part of the brain seizes on the thoughts and events that engaged its attention during the waking state; if the hypnotist could by delicate and skilful suggestion, provided the sleep were not too deep, establish *rapport* between the sleeper and himself, there seems great probability that the sleeper would be as susceptible to suggestion as any hypnotised subject. It is said that this experiment has been tried with success, and if this *rapport* could be clearly established in even a few cases, the essential alliance of the sleeping and the hypnotic state would seem to be proved. The exact point, however, is very difficult to hit upon. If the person be sleeping lightly the speech necessary in making the experiment would be likely to wake him; or, on the other hand, he would be insensible to any suggestion by reason of his deep sleep. In the few experiments of this nature that the writer has been able to make, he has met with some satisfactory but not conclusive results.

In the discussion of the various hypnotic states the reader will notice that there is one state—somnambulism—in which the subject, on awaking, has completely forgotten all that took place under the hypnosis; whilst, in the others, the memory is more or less complete.

These two states find their counterparts, also, in dreaming sleep. There seem to be in fact three phases of dreams—

1. Dreams, occurring most frequently in deep sleep, which, in the waking state, are quite forgotten.
2. Dreams remembered on waking.
3. Dreams in which the sleep is so light that they are not only remembered, but their unreality is recognised during the dream itself.

For all these curious facts, we find striking analogies in the various degrees of hypnosis. There is a more intense form of dream—sleep-walking, or somnambulism—which differs from the lighter forms in the fact that the dreamer not only thinks but acts. Here again there are many stages, from the one who mutters incoherent words to the deepest somnambulism with which most are familiar. The somnambulist can clearly see his way as he passes by, but he does not see any persons who may be watching him; nor does he hear words that are addressed to him. He is awake, apparently, only to perform the particular act which is in his mind. It is possible, however, for the somnambulist to hear words addressed to him if they have reference to the subject on which he is intent. The following, quoted from Dr Carpenter, is a case in point:—

"A young lady, when at school, frequently began to talk after having been asleep an hour or two; her ideas almost always ran upon the events of the previous day; and, if encouraged by leading questions addressed to her, she would give a very distinct and coherent account of them, frequently disclosing her own peccadilloes and those of her school-fellows, and expressing great penitence for the former, whilst she seemed to hesitate about making known the latter. To all ordinary sounds, however, she seemed perfectly insensible. A loud noise would awake her, but was never perceived in the sleep-talking state; and if the interlocutor addressed to her any questions or observations that did not fall in with her train of thought, they were completely disregarded. By a little adroitness, however, she might be led to talk upon almost any subject—a transition being *gradually* made from one to another by means of leading questions."

Perhaps the most important note of the somnambulic state is that nothing of the thought or action is remembered in the waking state, or is remembered only as a dream. Every particular, however, is often remembered on the next occasion.

Another case is quoted, by Carpenter, proving clearly this fact. "A servant-maid, rather given to sleep-walking, missed one of her combs; and being unable to discover it, on making the most diligent search, charged the fellow-servant, who slept in her room, with having taken it. One morning, however, she awoke *with the comb in her hand;* so that there can be no doubt that she had put it away on a previous night, without preserving any waking remembrance of the occurrence; and that she had recovered it when the remembrance of its hiding-place was brought to her by the recurrence of the state in which it had been secreted."

This recurrence of memory coincides precisely with the features of the hypnotic state, where the subject on awaking will know nothing of the experiments performed, but on the next hypnosis will remember them all.

Finally, I quote one of the most complete cases extant, recorded by Dr Abercombie on the authority of Dr James Gregory, and quoted by Carpenter. An officer who served in the expedition to Louisburgh in 1758 was subject to dreaming. The course of this individual's dreams could be completely directed by whispering into his ear, especially if this was done by a friend with whose voice he was familiar, and his companions in the transport were in the constant habit of amusing themselves at his expense. At one time they conducted him through the whole progress of a quarrel, which ended in a duel; and when the parties were supposed to be met, a pistol was put in his hand, which he fired, and was awakened by the report. On another occasion they found him asleep on the top of a locker in the cabin, when they made him believe he had fallen overboard, and exhorted him to save himself by swimming. He immediately imitated all the motions of swimming. They then told him that a shark was pursuing him, and entreated him to dive for his life. He instantly did so, with such force as to throw himself entirely from the locker upon the cabin floor, by which he was much bruised, and of course awakened. After the landing of the army at Louisburgh, his friends found him one day asleep in his tent, and evidently much annoyed by the cannonading. They then made him believe that he was engaged, when he expressed great fear, and showed an evident disposition to run away. Against this they remonstrated, but at the same time increased his fears, by imitating the groans of the wounded and dying; and when he asked, as he often did, who was down, they named his particular friends. At last they told him that the man next to himself in the line had fallen, when he instantly sprang from his bed, and was aroused from his danger and his dream together by falling over the tent ropes. After these experiments he had no distinct recollection of his dreams, but only a confused feeling of oppression and fatigue, and he used to tell his friends that he was sure they had been playing some trick upon him.

Liébault and Bernheim have all along maintained the close relationship of natural and hypnotic sleep, and their view seems to be confirmed by a large mass of evidence. Dr Moll and Dr Lloyd Tuckey, however, though they both adopt the methods and theories of Nancy, differ from this opinion. Tuckey says, " I cannot but think that Bernheim has somewhat exaggerated the closeness of the analogy between hypnotic and natural sleep," and unquestionably in the lighter forms of hypnosis the resemblance is not, at first sight, great ; but the fact of the subject's expectancy and of the artificial induction of the state may serve to explain the increased powers of the states compared with light natural sleep.

The next necessary consideration is the analogy of hypnotic suggestion to be found in the waking state.

The influence of the mind upon the body, to those who have studied at all the nervous system, seems no more wonderful than the influence which the body has over the mental state ; but the sudden physical changes which occur in response to a mental impression, often occasion surprise from the fact of the cause being a power so intangible and so little understood as the brain. The nature and the power of this influence varies greatly in individuals, but its common presence in all is demonstrated. Müller said that "Ideas do not act merely on the motor apparatus by which they are expressed; they as frequently affect the organs of sense, which then present sensorial impressions or images of the ideas." Herbert Spencer, by his own account, if he thought of seeing a slate rubbed by a sponge, experienced the same thrill that actually seeing it produces. The well-known tale of the butcher who, when getting down a joint of meat, fell and was caught up by the hook, is another instance. The hook, as a matter of fact, only passed through his coat; but he imagined that he was literally hung up by the flesh, and experienced, in consequence, the most acute agony. Dr Hack Tuke relates a curious illustration of the influence of the imagination upon sensorial impression, which occurred during the fire at the Crystal Palace in 1867. When the animals were destroyed by the fire, it was supposed that the chimpanzee had succeeded in escaping from his cage. Attracted to the roof with this expectation in full force, men saw the unhappy animal holding on to it, and writhing in agony to get astride one of the iron ribs. It need not be said that its struggles were watched by those below with breathless suspense and "sickening dread." But there was no animal whatever there, and all this feeling was thrown away upon a tattered piece of blind, so torn as to resemble to the eye of fancy the body, arms, and legs of an ape! Dr Tuckey quotes a case recorded by Woodhouse Braine, the chloroformist. The operator had placed the inhaling bag, without any ether or other anæsthetic, over the mouth and nose of the patient—a young girl—in order to familiarise her with the treatment. He was astonished to find that in a moment or two the patient was becoming unconscious; and, soon, her eyes turned up and she was perfectly insensible, and a painful operation was performed without the use of any anæsthetic. "Imagination" is a proper term to use in such cases, if it be properly understood; but it must be remembered that the effect is as real and just as much a fact when the nerve currents are sent from the brain to a particular part of the body, as when these currents are dispatched from that part of the body to the brain.

This is conclusively shown in the instances quoted, and, however wonderful or inexplicable it may seem to many, it cannot be denied that the imagination was sufficient to produce a state in which a most painful operation could be performed without in the least distressing the patient. But, in reality, the phenomenon is no more inexplicable than the ordinary and more normal action of the nerves, and for this reason I prefer the term "Ideation" to that of "Imagination," since the latter word, by its frequent use, in many different senses, is easily capable of misconstruction, and is likely, therefore, to be misleading. *Ideation* is the name given to a certain nerve centre, whose particular function is to adjust the action of the other nerve centres to an harmony with the requirements of the person and external circumstances. Other centres co-operate with it in this respect, but it is undoubtedly the faculty by which we form our opinions, appreciate and depreciate. It is, so to speak, the centre which receives the reports of the various other centres, and from their experiences deduces the proper act or thought. As a nerve centre can receive, so it can originate, for sensation must begin somewhere; and if, on the hand being pricked by a needle, the nerves in the hand can transmit the afferent currents to the brain, whilst, on these being received, a particular function of the brain will locate the position of the disturbance, it is not more wonderful that these centres themselves can originate, and this, in fact, is done when any movement of the body is made: thus it is only on a distinct nervous impulse from the motor centre that it is possible for the arm to be stretched out, the hand raised, or any other voluntary act performed.

It is possible, then, even in the normal waking state, for disease or cure to be induced by an active imagination. Similar results may be brought about by the suspension for the time of certain faculties, and especially of the inhibitory or restraining centre. It is well known that under circumstances of extreme fright acts have been performed which, under ordinary conditions, would never have been attempted. Men chased by bulls have jumped across streams, cleared hurdles, and accomplished athletic feats which, in their every-day life, they would have laughed at the idea of trying. Tuckey records the case of a young lady who had for months been confined to her bed, or couch, unable to walk a step, from apparent paralysis which defied all treatment. One morning news was brought that her brother, to whom she was devotedly attached, had fallen from his horse and was lying in a critical condition some miles away. She immediately got up, herself helped to saddle a horse, rode to the scene of the accident, and nursed her brother night and day for a week. The nervous shock had brought the volitional centre, or will, into operation, and she was permanently cured. Of the large number of electrical belts which are advertised few possess any electrical power, as any one with a slight knowledge of electricity can verify by a cursory examination. That many of them do good is almost equally undeniable, and this, so far from being wonderful, is only another evidence of the power of suggestion.

A friend was telling me recently of an experience which bears much on the present point. He went to bed feeling very ill, and his wife sent for the doctor. Instead of merely prescribing for his patient, the doctor sat by the bedside talking airily and lightly, and assuring him occasionally that he was really quite well. At the end of half-an-hour the doctor left, and my friend asked why the doctor had been sent for,—he felt perfectly well. A spell of mental fatigue and worry had resulted in a mild attack of nervous prostration, which the skilful suggestion of the doctor had been sufficient to dissipate.

Many more instances might be adduced, but those quoted are sufficient to illustrate the influence of suggestion on the nervous, and consequently on the physical, system.

It may be said, however, that the practice of this suggestion in the case of weak-minded persons is no doubt of value, but that it is unlikely to be applicable to one possessed of a really healthy mind and body. In reality, every one is influenced by suggestion; in the case of one with no great strength of will, a word or an act may be sufficient to attain the purpose, whilst a healthy mind will generally only respond to a more hidden and a more subtle impulse. What is it that so imbues the mind of the Conservative with his principles, that he completely fails to appreciate the qualities and doctrines of his opponents? And why such contempt in the Liberal for the ideas of Conservatism?

Training, education, environment, in the large majority of cases, account for the political and other views of men. All these are but forms of suggestion, emphasised, possibly, at no given time with any great insistence, but, year by year, engrafted on the mind.

The influence which a learned and patient scholar will exert over many of his listeners and readers is of a similar nature.

The most successful leaders of thought are those who best know how to "suggest" by a subtle combination of the tentative and the dogmatic.

Thus, there seems to be in the human organism a dual nervous action, the one automatic and intuitive, the other rational, volitional, and deliberative.[1] They may act separately, or together, as circumstances demand. Generally, walking, seeing, hearing are automatic actions in which no exercise of the will is necessary; nor can it be said that, though the action of the will is not felt, it may, nevertheless, be necessary to, and acting in, these "automatic" acts. Such an hypothesis is not applicable to the involuntary movements of the hand or arm, often made on the impulse of the moment, to be checked the next moment by the action of the reasoning and deliberative centres; and it is not possible to allow of any volitional act in the performance of the organic function of respiration. Whilst the action of these two parts of the nervous system—the

[1] *Vide* Tuckey, *op. cit.*

automatic and the rational—is frequently distinct, it is almost equally common for the two to be working in harmony, leading thereby to increased functional power.

By the concentration of the attention and the will, a small or distant object can be discerned, which otherwise would be indistinct; and similarly, sound may be heard by concentration or expectant attention, which, but for this, would escape the ear. Many, when working at some difficult problem, are accustomed to close their eyes for several moments, and this instinctive action leads to greater power in the other centres.

It is well known that the constant use of any one sense by such concentration will lead to increased automatic function of that sense. The extraordinary extent to which these powers may be increased in abnormal conditions of the waking state is exemplified by the fine senses of touch and hearing developed in the blind. An interesting case of increased faculties in such an one has been recently communicated to me by a lady. The blind man is an adept organist; by the difference of sound, which his footstep makes, he can tell when he is approaching a tree or a lamp-post, and can distinguish between them. In the same way he will distinguish between an house, a wall, or railings. By the sound of his voice he knows whether the door of a room be open or shut. The senses of touch and smell are developed to an equally great extent, till it would seem that he could hardly do more had he the use of his sight.

The intellect is capable of producing sensation —increasing the sensation to an abnormal degree, or suspending it altogether. Instances of the production, increase, or suspension of sensation are to be found in large numbers. All three may occur in the same individual at different times, but it is more often found that the individual is subject to only one of these intellectual influences.

Braid records an experiment of his bearing on this. He requested four gentlemen in good health to lay their arms on a table with the palm of their hand upwards. Each was to look at the palm of his hand for a few minutes with fixed attention, and watch the result. In about five minutes the first, a member of the Royal Academy, stated that he felt a sensation of great cold in the hand ; another, who was an author of note, said that for some time he thought nothing was going to happen, but at last he experienced a darting, pricking sensation in the palm of the hand, as if electric sparks were being drawn from it ; the third gentleman, who had been mayor of a large borough, said that he felt a very uncomfortable sensation of heat come over his hand ; the fourth, secretary to an important association, had become rigidly cataleptic, his arm being firmly fixed to the table.

The noticeable point about this experiment is that

Braid made no suggestion that there should be any sensation, and in trying experiments of this kind I have frequently sought to find some connection between the intellectual disposition of the individual and the nature of the sensation experienced. In young women of good mental capacity and of sensitive disposition, the arm will most frequently become cataleptic; in men and women of brilliant capacity, the arm generally becomes rigid, or they feel a sensation often described as "pricking," but more often as "very strange"; whilst in those of somewhat lower mental order, but of a more even temperament, heat or cold is most commonly felt. The explanation seems to lie in the fact that the blood supply of a part will be increased if attention is devoted to that part.

John Hunter said, "I am confident that I can fix my attention to any part until I have a sensation in that part"; and any doctor, when testing the condition of the heart, will seek to distract the attention of his patients from that organ. The fact of this increased flow of the blood does not, however, explain the varying nature of the sensations, nor the catalepsy, and it is probable that the sense of constriction, due to the excess of blood, acts as a suggestion *per se* in persons of "electric" or sensitive nature, resulting in partial or complete inhibition of the motor nerves. This seems the only possible explanation of the catalepsy; but there are other explanations applicable to the simple sensation. The constant changes which take place in the tissue are unobserved by the individual in normal circumstances; but it is not impossible that on the attention being directed to a particular part, those processes may, to a certain extent, affect the consciousness, and thus form an inherent suggestion. Reichenbach imagined he had discovered a new power which he termed the "Odic" force. This power he found to proceed from magnets, and he elaborated his theories with much evidence. Braid investigated these discoveries, and found that, drawing a magnet or other object from the wrist to the point of the fingers produced nearly always some effect. The persons would experience a change of temperature, tingling, creeping, pricking, etc., whilst when he drew the magnet from the fingers to the wrist, it was generally followed by a change of sensation from the altered current of ideas suggested by the reversed motion. In order to satisfy himself that these were all due entirely to suggestion, Braid requested his patient to look aside, or interposed a screen, and if they were requested to describe their sensations during the repetition of the processes, similar symptoms were realised when there was nothing done beyond watching them and noting their responses. Braid quotes another case. The patient was a lady, whom he placed in a dark room and then requested her to look at the poles of a powerful horse-shoe magnet, and to describe what she saw. After some time she declared that she saw nothing. He then told her to look attentively and she would see fire come out of it. She soon saw sparks, and after a little time, in great numbers. The trunk which contained the magnet was then closed but she still saw the sparks. Making the suggestion to her, by leading questions, Braid asked her to describe what she saw from another part of the room, where there was nothing but bare walls, when she described the most brilliant coruscations.

Dr Wigan records a striking instance which occurred within his own experience. He was attending a soirée given in Paris by M. Bellart, shortly after the execution of Marshal Ney, which had created a profound impression at the time. On the arrival of a visitor, M. Maréchal *aîné*, he was announced as Maréchal Ney. Dr Wigan said that an electric shudder ran through the company, and the resemblance of the prince was, for a moment, as perfect to his eyes as if it had been the reality. With reference to this instance, as a confirmation of the fact that whilst the illusion is due to the imagination, it is not in the ordinary sense imaginative, Herbert Spencer may be quoted:—" Those vivid states of consciousness which we know as sensations, accompany direct, and therefore strong, excitations of nerve-centres ; while the faint states of consciousness which we know as remembered sensations, or ideas of sensations, accompany indirect, and therefore weak, excitation of the same nerve-centres."

John Hunter said that "every part of the body sympathises with the mind, for whatever affects the mind, the body is affected in proportion." That this is so is confirmed by universal experience.

Every human passion is betrayed in action when, apparently, such action is quite unnecessary. At a public meeting, where keen interest is aroused, the various emotions depicted on the faces of the audience, present an entrancing study. The movements made in private conversation, often quite involuntary, and always in harmony with the thoughts and utterances of the speaker, betray to an extent, frequently unappreciated, the subtle inter-action of the various nerve-centres. Not only does the intellect possess and use an enormous influence over the sensations and voluntary actions, but the organic functions are equally affected by it.

So frequently have eminent specialists died from the disease which has been their particular study that the explanation of coincidence is too weak to account for the facts. One of the most curious instances recorded is that of a medical student in Paris, who was being initiated into the mystic rites of a Masonic society. His eyes were bandaged, a ligature bound round his arm, and the usual preparations made to bleed him. When a pretence of opening the vein was made, a stream of water was spurted into a bowl, the sound of which resembled that of the flow of blood which the student was anticipating. The consequence was that in a few moments he became pale and before long fainted away.

Perhaps the strongest and most patent testimony of the Influence of the Mind on the Body is to be found in hysterical cases. These cases present the greatest difficulty to physicians, as in nearly all of them the patient is systematically bent on deceiving, and endeavours by all the means in her (for hysteria is a disease of which women practically maintain a monopoly) power to exaggerate the symptoms. In cases of hysteria it is well known that the patient neither goes into fits nor faints unless there be some one present. In serious cases, however, the disease is more real, and Dr Hammond describes it as " a paralysis of the will."

An hysterical patient [1] will suddenly take to her bed and declare she has no feeling and no power in her arms or legs. The most careful examination shows that she is speaking the truth. Pins may be thrust into the limb, it may be punctured or scorched, and yet the patient neither winces nor betrays the least sign of pain. Analogies of such a state are to be found in ordinary life; when, by excitement or some disturbing influence the brain is

[1] This and other cases are taken from "Spiritualism and Nervous Derangement." Hammond.

working at such a high strain as to be beyond its inhibitory and volitional control. Soldiers engaged in a furious battle have been seriously wounded and have fought on, unconscious of either pain or injury, and, still more frequently, in the midst of a game, an injury has been received, of which the player is conscious, but, till his excitement has cooled down, he has not had the power to locate the injured part. The extraordinary treatment to which hysterical persons can be subjected without their experiencing any ill effects, almost baffles comprehension.

Montgeron[1] relates that many women who visited the tomb of the Abbé Paris gave themselves blows with instruments in such a manner that the sharp points were forced into the flesh. Fouillon[2] states that another had herself hung up by the heels with the head downwards, and remained in that position three-quarters of an hour. One day, as she lay extended on her bed, two men who held a cloth under her back, raised her up and threw her forward two thousand four hundred times, while two other persons placed in front, thrust her back. Another day, four men, having taken hold of her by the extremities, began to pull her, each with all his strength, and she was thus dragged in different directions for the space of some minutes. She

---

[1] La Vérité des Miracles, quoted by Hammond, op. cit.
[2] Quoted by Hammond, op. cit.

caused herself to be tied as she lay on the table, her arms crossed behind her back, and her legs flexed to their fullest extent, and, while six men struck her without ceasing, a seventh choked her. After this she remained insensible for some time, and her tongue, inflamed and discoloured, hung far out of her mouth. Another insisted upon receiving an hundred blows upon the abdomen with an hand-iron, and these were so heavy that they shook the wall against which she was placed, and upon one occasion a breach in it was caused at the twenty-fifth blow.

A physician, hearing of these things, insisted that they could not be true, as it was physically impossible that the skin, the flesh, the bones and the internal organs, could resist such violence. He was told to come and verify the facts. He hastened to do so, and was struck with astonishment. Scarcely believing his eyes, he begged to be allowed to adminster the blows. A strong iron instrument, sharp at one end, was put into his hands; he struck with all his might and thrust it deep into the flesh, but the victim laughed at his efforts, and remarked that his blows only did her good.

Besides these Dr Hammond relates some cases of his own experience. A young woman, a patient in the wards of the Pennsylvania Hospital, began a series of movements, which consisted in bending her body backwards till it formed an arch, her heels and head alone resting on the bed, and then suddenly straightening herself out, she would fall heavily. Instantly the arch was formed again; again she fell; and this process was kept up with inconceivable rapidity for several hours every day. In another instance, a lady, during an attack of hysterical paroxysms to which she was liable, beat her head with such violence against a lath and plaster partition, that she made a hole in it, while little or no injury was inflicted on herself. In another, a girl, eighteen years of age, lay down on the floor and made all the members of her family stand on her in turn. A lady, in order that she might resemble those martyrs who suffered on the rack, tied her wrists with a stout cord, mounted a step-ladder, fastened the cord to a hook in the wall, and jumping from the ladder succeeded in dislocating her shoulder. Another lady rigidly closed her mouth, and refused to open it either to take food or to speak for over forty-eight hours. No force, that it was safe to use, could overcome the contraction of her muscles, and no persuasion induce her to relax them. She only yielded to an irresistible impulse to talk, and to a degree of hunger that human nature could no longer endure.

In the sixteenth and seventeenth centuries several convents in Europe were afflicted with an epidemic of hysteria. Such diseases are greatly increased by virtue of the imitative faculty, and many nuns were suffering from fearful convulsions and cataleptic paroxysms. The nuns of Loudon are a notable case. In these times "demoniacal possession" was believed in, as of not infrequent occurrence, and, in fact, many of the nuns in their hysterical attacks accused persons of bewitching them.

The nature of the phenomena is shown in a series of curious questions put to the University of Montpellier by Fr. Santerre.

1. Whether the bending, bowing, and removing of the body, the head touching sometimes the soles of the feet, with other contortions and strange postures, are a good sign of possession?
2. Whether the quickness of the motion of the head forwards and backwards, bringing it to the back and the breast, be an infallible mark of possession?
3. Whether a sudden swelling of the tongue, the throat, and the face, and the sudden alteration of the colour, are certain marks of possession?
4. Whether dulness and senselessness, or the privation of sense, even to be pinched and pricked without complaining, without stirring, and even without changing colour, are certain marks of possession?
5. Whether the immobility of the whole body which happens to the pretended possessed, by the command of their exorcists during and in the middle of the strongest agitations, be a certain sign of a truly diabolical possession?

6. Whether the yelping or barking like that of a dog, in the breast rather than in the throat, be a mark of possession?
7. Whether a fixed, steady look upon some object, without moving the eye on either side, be a good mark of possession?
8. Whether the answers that the pretended possessed made in French, to some questions that are put to them in Latin, are a good mark of possession?
9. Whether to vomit such things as people have swallowed be a sign of possession?
10. Whether the prickings of a lancet upon divers parts of the body, without blood issuing thence are a certain mark of possession?

In addition to these cases on the Continent, a similar form of hysteria was prevalent in America, instances of which Hammond records. They, however, did not last long. Mather writes that "Experience showed that the more these were apprehended the more were still afflicted by Satan, and the number of confessions increasing did but increase the number of the accused; and the executing of some made way for the apprehending of others. For still the afflicted complained of being tormented by new objects, as the former were removed. So that those who were concerned grew amazed at the number and quality of the persons accused, and feared that Satan by his wiles had enwrapped innocent persons under the imputation of that crime ; and at last it was evidently seen that there must be a stop put, or the generation of the children of God would fall under that condemnation. Henceforth, therefore, the juries generally acquitted such as were tried, fearing they had gone too far before, and Sir William Phips, the governor, reprieved all that were condemned, even the confessors as well as others."

That such changes in the human organism are possible would be difficult to believe, were they not testified to by witnesses without number, whilst in the hospitals to-day similar cases are to be met with ; though, with the progress of knowledge and science, the diseases are generally met, to some extent, in their early stages, and prevented from assuming the proportions which were common in earlier times.

The striking fact is, that, in the majority of these cases, the mental faculties are in other ways unimpaired. Many of these epileptics and convulsionaires were even brilliant in their gifts and conversation. The mere suspension of the volitional centre was sufficient to account for these, at first sight, unaccountable states.

Slight reference has already been made to the influence which powerful speakers or learned scholars may exert over the minds of those who are listening to them ; such influence, so far from indicating any lack of power or strength in the hearer, may be an evidence of the hearer's fine perception and delicate taste. Indeed, without the constant interaction which is the result of human thought, life would be a dreary monotony. The suggestion, however, often hidden under this power or influence, may frequently bear with such force on persons as to entirely overcome the volitional and rational centres. They become imbued with an idea, which is the ruling passion, and no exterior circumstances can affect, or will be noticed, by them.

This state may occur in men and women of high mental calibre, and in fact is more likely to occur in such. It is no infrequent experience to hear persons say that, in listening to some performance of music or a drama at the theatre, for the time they quite "lost themselves," and one has only to watch their countenance at such a time to find its conclusive verification. External circumstances have lost all hold of them. They are entirely dominated by the idea which has been presented to them; external consciousness is absent, and, often, shaking, or some other more or less violent means, has to be resorted to, in order to bring them back, once more, into touch with the outer world. One has only to study many of the convulsive religious movements to notice this influence exerted to such an extent that the devotees are absolutely beyond all reason and control. In India it is well known that there are many sects who, by the practice of strange arts, reduce themselves to conditions in which they are able to perform feats that fill the onlooker with amazement. The Fakirs and others have filled the spectator with wonder and awe by many of their performances; though, by the testimony of critical observers, it seems as if, with regard to the Fakir, the human tendency to exaggerate is responsible for some of the tales told of them. The Aïssouans are a powerful religious sect in Morocco, and some of them were to be seen performing in London recently. I quote from the description of an eye-witness:—

"These Aïssouans bring on themselves a sort of delirium by dances and the repetition of special litanies chanted in chorus and by inhaling perfumes of a particular quality, the whole being accompanied by music of a strange and weird character. At first they all sit round, looking grave and with an air of thorough conviction. Each Aïssuoan performs in his turn; and then after an harum-scarum dance, without rhyme or rhythm, followed by disorderly leaps and bounds, they all howl and the music ceases. Each actor seems to feel a divine inspiration, and to be ready to dare and accomplish anything. These Aïssouans, one by one, exhibited such specimens as the above of the manners of their country, before a crowd of spectators. One of them might be seen eating the thorny, leathery leaves of the cactus; another piercing his cheeks, tongue, neck and arms, with long thick iron needles attached to heavy balls; another would greedily devour scorpions and live snakes; another would crack with his teeth, apparently with great gusto, sharp fragments of glass; a head man of the tribe licked a red-hot shovel and forced his eye out of its socket; —and all this was repeated over and over again.

"The Aïssouan will tear and lacerate his skin scarcely making the blood run, and, while thus torturing himself, he will leap, bound, howl, and then salute his companions on the forehead and sit down gravely. He will let his stomach be pierced with long nails driven in with a mallet by one of his co-religionists; and not content with crunching glass with his jaws, and devouring it, he will swallow whole pebbles, devour living vipers, or make them bite with undisguised satisfaction."[1]

These, however, are probably forms of hypnotism induced by the fatigue or the drugs they inhale. Tuckey says that they are hypnotised by their priest before the performance.

There are many instances in modern times, in England, of the power of unhealthy suggestion on persons of morbid intellect.

The following is taken from the diary of Wesley:—

"*Sunday, May* 20.—Being with Mr B—ll, at Everton, I was much fatigued and did not rise, but Mrs B— did, and observed many fainting and crying

---

[1] Foveau de Courmelles. *Hypnotism*, p. 169.

out while Mr Beveridge was preaching; afterwards, at church, I heard many cry out, especially children, whose agonies were amazing; one of the oldest, a girl of ten or twelve years old, was full in my view, in violent contortions of body, and weeping aloud, I think, incessantly during the whole service, and several much younger children were in Mr B—ll's full view, agonizing as they did. The church was equally crowded in the afternoon, the windows being filled within and without, and even the outside of the pulpit to the very top, so that Mr B— seemed almost stifled with their breathing, yet feeble and sickly as he is, he was continually strengthened, and his voice, for the most part, distinguishable in the midst of all the outcries. I believe there were present three times more men than women, a greater part of whom came from afar; thirty of them having set out at two in the morning, from a place thirteen miles off. The text was:—'Having a fear of godliness, but denying the power thereof.' When the power of religion began to be spoken of, the presence of God really filled the place; and while poor sinners felt the sentence of death in their souls, what sounds of distress did I hear! The greatest number of those who cried or fell, were men; but some women and several children felt the power of the same Almighty Spirit, and seemed just sinking into hell. This occasioned a mixture of various sounds; some shrieking, some roaring aloud. The most general was a loud breathing like that of people half-strangled and gasping for life; and indeed, almost all the cries were like those of human creatures dying in bitter anguish. Great numbers wept without any noise; others fell down as dead; some sinking in silence; some with extreme noise and agitation. I stood on the pew seat, as did a young man on the opposite pew, an able-bodied, fresh, healthy countryman; but in a moment, while he seemed to think of nothing less, down he dropped with a violence inconceivable. The adjoining pew seemed to shake with his fall. I heard afterwards the stamping of his feet; ready to break the boards as he lay in strong convulsions at the bottom of the pew. Among several that were struck down in the next pew, was a girl who was as violently seized as he. When he fell, Mr B—ll and I felt our souls thrilled with a momentary dread; as when one man is killed with a cannon-ball another often feels the wind of it.

"Among the children who felt the arrows of the Almighty, I saw a sturdy boy, about eight years old, who roared above his fellows, and seemed, in his agony, to struggle with the strength of a grown man. His face was red as scarlet, and almost all on whom God laid His hand, turned either very red or almost black. When I returned, after a little walk, to Mr Beveridge's house, I found it full of people. He was fatigued, but said he would nevertheless give them a word of exhortation. I stayed in the next room, and saw the girl whom I had observed so peculiarly distressed in the church lying on the floor as one dead, but without any ghastliness in her face. In a few minutes we were informed of a woman filled with peace and joy, who was crying out just before. She had come thirteen miles, and is the same person who dreamed Mr B— would come to her village on that day whereon he did come, though without either knowing the place or the way to it. She was convinced at that time. Just as we heard of her deliverance, the girl on the floor began to stir. She was then set on a chair, and, after sighing awhile, suddenly rose up rejoicing in God. Her face was covered with the most beautiful smile I ever saw. She frequently fell on her knees, but was generally running to and fro, speaking these and the like words: 'Oh, what can Jesus do for lost sinners? He has forgiven all my sins! I am in heaven! I am in heaven! Oh, how He loves *me!* And how I love Him.' Meantime I saw a thin, pale girl, weeping with sorrow for herself and joy for her companion. Quickly the smiles of heaven came likewise on her, and her praises joined with those of the other. I also then laughed with extreme joy, so did Mr B—ll (who said it was more than he could well bear). So did all who knew the Lord, and some of those who were waiting for salvation, till the cries of those who were struck with the arrows of conviction were almost lost in the sounds of joy. . . . Immediately after a stranger, well-dressed, who stood facing me, fell backward to the wall; then forward on his knees, wringing his hands, and roaring like a bull. His face at first turned quite red, and then almost black. He rose and ran against the wall, till Mr Keeling and another held him. He screamed out, 'Oh, what shall I do, what shall I do? Oh, for one drop of the blood of Christ!' As he spoke, God set his soul at liberty; he knew his sins were blotted out; and the raptures he was in seemed too great for human nature to bear. He had come forty miles to hear Mr B—, and was to leave the next morning; which he did with a glad heart, telling all who came in his way what God had done for his soul. . . . And now did I see such a sight as I do not expect again on this side eternity. The faces of the three justified children, and I think of all the believers present, did really shine; and such a beauty, such a look of extreme happiness, and, at the same time, of divine love and simplicity, did I never see in human faces till now. The newly justified eagerly embraced one another, weeping on each others' necks for joy. Then they saluted all of their own sex, and besought men and women to help them in praising God."

Another curious instance of the suspension of the rational centres is to be found in "Shakerism."

I quote some instances. Mother Ann (the presiding genius of the order) is supposed to have a splendid vineyard; the walks are of pure gold, with angels walking around among the vines. There are ten thousand kinds of grapes. Mother Ann superintends her own wine press, and often brings wine ("spiritual") as a present. The visionist pretends to take a waiter filled with wine-glasses; everybody must have faith, and take one as it is handed to them. Those who have little or no faith are told by the visionist whether they have taken theirs. Then they all raise their hands to their lips as in the act of drinking, and presently they begin to reel and stagger round the room as though actually drunk. Indeed, they act in all respects as drunken persons, stamping, shaking, vomiting, etc., till finally exhausted, they gradually sink away till all is silent. Then, standing in a circle, they throw their handkerchiefs over their shoulders, raise their hands to their heads, and make six solemn bows, saying with each, "I kindly thank Mother for this beautiful gift." A gift, sometimes called the "mortification gift," enters the room. The inspired immediately begin slapping their hands against their sides, and crowing in imitation of a chicken cock. Some will cackle, others imitate the turkey, duck, hen, goose, or guinea-fowl.

Sometimes young men and women are exercised

by what they call the "jerks" for two weeks at a time, during the whole of which period the head is kept in continual motion by quick convulsive motions of the shoulders and neck. One young woman who had been "jerked" for three weeks had her face frightfully swollen, and her eyes dilated and bloodshot.

Directly after the "jerks" she began to talk in unknown tongues, and continued, at short intervals, for three or four days; then she stopped suddenly and remained entirely mute for two weeks, no possible persuasion being sufficient to make her say even "yes" or "no." This experience is called the "dumb devils."[1]

I have endeavoured to give in these various instances an example of the numerous phases of suggestive influence which can be brought to bear in the waking state. In order to render it as complete as possible, I have not hesitated to include in the category many strange and unhealthy forms of this power; but it must be noted that the unhealthiness of these symptoms lies in the fact that the brains of such persons are, *in the waking state*, open to such influence. It is evident that under chloroform and ether, persons are reduced to a condition which would indeed be serious were it to occur spontaneously, under normal conditions, without the administration of any anæsthetic or

[1] Hammond. Op. cit., p. 243 *et seq.*

drug; but it is no reflection on hypnotism that similiar states as those that have been described could be produced under hypnosis. For were this otherwise, the peculiar value of hypnotism in the cure of functional and nervous disorders would disappear.

It has been already explained that these strange phenomena were due to the suspension of the volitional centre; this being suspended, the whole of the nervous system is dependent for its action upon the ideas that are impressed upon it, and acts upon those ideas without any control or restraint by reason of the inhibition of those centres which can only give the necessary controlling power. The persons subject to these religous convulsions, which have been referred to, are amenable to no ordinary medical treatment; but hypnotism, with the facility it gives the operator of increasing the power and the force of the weakened nerve-centres, is capable of completely curing many such cases of hysteria.

There are many subtle forms of suggestion which have not been touched in this chapter, but which are curious and interesting as examples of its action in the normal and perfectly healthy waking state. Dr Ochorowicz[1] relates an experiment which I have tried under similiar circumstances, often with success. He shall tell it in his own words:—

[1] Mental Suggestion, p. 20

"My friend P., a man no less absent-minded than he is keen of intellect, was playing chess in a neighbouring room. Others of us were talking near the door. I had made the remark that it was my friend's habit, when he paid closest attention to the game to whistle an air from 'Madame Angot.' I was about to accompany him by beating time on the table; but this time he whistled something else—the march from 'Le Prophète.'

"'Listen,' said I to my associates; 'we are going to play a trick upon P. We will mentally order him to pass from "Le Prophète" to "La Fille de Madame Angot."'

"First I began to drum the march; then, profiting by some notes common to both, I passed quickly to the quicker and more *staccato* measure of my friend's favourite air. P. on his part also suddenly changed the air, and began to whistle 'Madame Angot.' Everyone burst out laughing. My friend was too much absorbed in a check to the queen to notice anything. 'Let us begin again,' said I, 'and go back to "Le Prophète."'

"And straightway we had Meyerbeer once more with a special fugue."

It is an amusing experiment to stand somewhere in a public thoroughfare, whilst a friend looks intently on some imaginary object on the path. Some passers-by will casually look round; more will stop to find what it is the friend is looking at; whilst not a few will be pulled up instantaneously as though they were paralysed.

In this chapter have been placed before the reader a number of instances, drawn from various sources, of mental action. These have been collected, not with the object of supporting any particular theory, but in the endeavour to illustrate the extent of the workings of the brain. If this be properly appreciated we are the better able to regard the state produced by hypnotism as one of the many mental and physiological states, and not as something absolutely unique.

In every state of the human organism conditions are to be found where, by action on the Ideational centre of the nervous system, effects are produced in which we can detect many of the characteristics of hypnosis, and we therefore conclude that the hypnotic state is not due to any impalpable and intangible exercise of will-power, or other influence, on the part of the hypnotist, but is a physiological adaptation of the brain of the hypnotised subject.

CHAPTER IV.

THE INDUCTION OF HYPNOSIS.

Hypnosis not an unnatural state—Telepathy—Clairvoyance—The methods of inducing hypnosis—The Mesmeric—Braid's—Passes—Berger's—Fascination—Lasegue's—Faria's—Magnets—Drugs—Luy's miroir rotatif—The Nancy method—The methods of waking—Danger of subject not waking—Duration of hypnotic sleep—Susceptibility to hypnotism—Van Eeden—Wetterstrand—Tuckey—Forel—Liébault—The stages of hypnotism—Gurney—Forel—Tuckey—Liébault—Bernheim—The school of Charcot—The difference of the two schools—The "New Mesmerism" and the Paris school.

IT is clear that the doctrines signified by the terms "mesmerism," "animal magnetism," "electrobiology," and the like, were incapable of any serious scientific study, since they concerned a state which, on these theories, was altogether incomprehensible if not supernatural; whether true or untrue, they may be said to stand much in the same position towards the scientific world as Spiritualism and Theosophy. By hypnotists it is claimed that this state, whether it be called mesmeric, magnetic, or what not, is one purely physiological and subjective, and this theory has been adhered to by almost all scientists, who have studied the question, since Braid first propounded it.

There are many interesting questions, such as Telepathy, Thought-reading, Clairvoyance, etc., upon which it would be perhaps rash to give any decided opinion; but it must be said that the hypnotic state *per se* has nothing to do with any of these phenomena. If telepathy be possible between two persons, it is by no means unlikely that the power would still exist, or even be increased under hypnosis.

All these strange psychical conditions present problems of the deepest interest; and if I do not attempt to deal with them here, it is not because they do not repay the time taken in their study, but because they have not a sufficient bearing on the normal states of hypnosis to justify a discussion of them.

The methods of inducing hypnosis are many and various, and I proceed to enumerate the ones principally used.[1]

[1] It may be well to define several terms which will be frequently used in the course of this book. I have carefully avoided all technical terms, as far as possible; but the few appended are necessary for brevity and clearness.

HYPNOTISM. The science which treats of the condition which is called "hypnosis." It denies that there is any truth in the theories known as "animal magnetism," "mesmerism," etc., and is founded on the theory that the state is simply a super-normal condition of the brain.

HYPNOSIS (Greek ὕπνος, sleep). The state produced by means of hypnotism, and which was formerly called the "magnetic" or "mesmeric" sleep. It is admitted that the term hypnosis, meaning, as it does, "sleep," does not adequately represent by its derivation the state produced, since many who are undoubtedly hypnotised are

I.

THE MESMERIC METHODS. As we have seen in the first chapter, Mesmer did not rely on any one method, but made use of numerous contrivances by means of which he sought to influence his patients. The essential point was that the patient should be in contact with the magnetiser or the magnetised *baquet*, in order that the "fluid" might pass into the patient's body.

BRAID'S METHOD. Braid placed some object before and slightly above the eyes of his patient. He then commanded him to gaze fixedly at this object, and to concentrate his attention on it. Dr Ernst Jendrásik of Buda-Pesth has expressed the opinion that fixed attention is only effective because it causes fatigue of the nerves of sight, and consequently produces insensibility to external sense-stimulation. It is known that for the induction

---

perfectly conscious and remember, on returning to the normal state, everything that has occurred during the time they were in hypnosis. Yet it is difficult, if not impossible, to find any word which would adequately represent the condition induced; and so long as we clearly understand what is meant by the term "hypnosis," we can afford to leave on one side the question of its derivative meaning. The essential characteristic of the hypnosis is not sleep, but *an heightened and increased receptivity of suggestion*.

HYPNOTIST. The one who scientifically induces hypnosis.

HYPNOTEE, HYPNOTIC, SUBJECT, are words used to signify the person hypnotised. "Subject" is the one most frequently used.

HYPNOTIC SUGGESTION. Any suggestion or impression given to the patient by the hypnotist either in words, writing, or in any manner which the subject can appreciate.

HYPNOGENESIS, *hypnosigenesis*, *hypnogeny*. All ugly words sometimes used to signify the induction of hypnosis.

of ordinary sleep it is not necessary that all the functions of the brain should be tired, and that if any one be sufficiently wearied sleep will ensue. The strained position of the eyes, and their convergence, under Braid's method, would undoubtedly soon fatigue the optic nerve, and thus sleep would be induced. Braid used solely this method, and he was remarkably successful.

PASSES. On these great importance was placed by the early magnetisers, and we find the most minute directions given for their correct application and use. The "pass" proper, however, was never used by Mesmer, to whom it was unknown. Generally, the operator gazed fixedly into the eyes of the subject as long as he continued to make the passes. The will was held to be an essential element, and it was necessary for the cure that the operator should strongly exercise his will that the nerve-force might the more easily pass into the body of the patient. These passes were divided into two kinds, "positive" and "negative." If they were used for the purpose of enveloping the patient in an healthy magnetism, they were "positive"; if they were intended to withdraw the unhealthy magnetism from the patient's body, they were then termed "negative." The mesmeric quacks of to-day profess great belief in the efficacy of these various passes, and, in a book before me, I find described and illustrated :—" The Reverse or Upward Pass for demesmerising," " The Curative Magnetic Pass for Toothache, Neuralgia, Rheumatism," etc., "The Curative Magnetic Pass for Spinal Complaints," etc. This is, of course, pure nonsense, but several hypnotists claim that the method of simple passes is often very valuable. Ch. Richet, Professor of Physiology at the University of Paris, uses this method in preference to any other. I have found it very effective in many cases. The precise nature of the action of these passes is difficult to determine. Unquestionably, the element of suggestion enters in, but it is doubtful whether this can account for all the results. It has been suggested that the difference of temperature between the hands of the operator and the face of the patient may cause a strange sensation, and thus induce an inhibitory action in the delicate nerves of the eye and of the mouth.

BERGER'S METHOD. Professor Oskar Berger of Breslau has stated that in some cases he found that warmth alone was sufficient to induce hypnosis, and that in a few instances it was only necessary to warm his hands and hold them near the head of the subject.

This theory rather supports the explanation of the passes which has been suggested above. Another hypothesis is that electrical action is caused. Dr Jean de Tarchanoff has shown that systematic gentle stimulations of the skin produce slight currents of electricity in it, and also that these currents can be produced by a strong concentration of the will, in consequence of which concentration, muscular contraction always ensues. The mesmerists held, as the result of their observations, that a strong volitional effort was necessary, and the experiments of Tarchanoff may serve to explain the value of this exertion of the will.

Professor A. Pitres of Bordeaux states that certain portions of the body are more particularly sensitive to stimulation of the skin. These parts he terms "zones hypnogènes," and a continuous stimulus applied to any one of these parts is said to produce hypnosis in some persons. Professor H. Spitta of Tübingen, and Professor J. Purkinge of Breslau and Prague, have testified to the influence of gentle friction of the forehead, and several subjects have told me that their sleep was deepened by this stroking of the forehead, which I have made use of in many cases.

Professor Adolph Weinhold of Chemnitz has made use of the electric battery, and claims the same results from it as from mesmeric passes; though he does not consider that suggestion is excluded.

Professor Albert Eulenburg, by galvanising the head, succeeded in obtaining a lethargic condition; this experiment, however, was not very convincing, as the patient had already suffered from attacks of lethargy. The mental element is certainly not excluded in these cases of electrisation; and Professor

Hirt of Breslau, whilst he constantly uses electricity in this way, is quite positive that it is not the galvanic current but the mental influence which causes the hypnosis.

FASCINATION. This method, introducing as it does a large amount of the personal element, is a favourite one of the mesmeric "professors." The subject is told to gaze steadily into the operator's eyes. It frequently happens that in a short space of time the subject will imitate every movement of the operator, all the while keeping his eyes firmly fixed on those of the operator. This method is somewhat risky, since, if the subject be refractory, the operator himself may involuntarily become hypnotised.

Dr Lloyd Tuckey records an instance where, in using this method on one occasion, he found himself developing the first symptoms of hypnosis.

LASEGUE'S METHOD. Dr Ch. Lasegue, a physician of Paris, found that closing the eyes and then making a moderate pressure on the eyeballs for some minutes often induced the state.

FARIA'S METHOD. The Abbé Faria used to concentrate the attention of his subject as much as possible, and after some minutes of perfect silence, would suddenly shout in a loud and commanding voice the word "sleep." In many cases this was sufficient to obtain the desired result.

A sudden fright often causes a temporary paralysis; indeed, the fatal railway accidents would be less in number if it were not for this phenomenon of sudden and intense fear. I recently saw a young man run over by a runaway horse. He had plenty of time to get out of the way, but apparently became fascinated, and remained fixed in the centre of the road until he was knocked down.

MAGNETS. Several authorities claim that the magnet has in some cases the power of hypnotising. Ballet, Binet et Féré, Landowzy and Proust, all of Paris, and Benedikt of Vienna, hold this view. In none of my own experiments have I been able to find any trace of such influence, and I find that this result is confirmed by the almost universal testimony of hypnotists in all parts of the world. It may be that in a certain few abnormal cases the magnet has this virtue; but it seems a more natural hypothesis to attribute these few hypnoses to suggestion, an element which enters into nearly every method, and which is so subtle in its action that it is almost impossible for an operator to state positively that it has been entirely avoided. Braid has left on record an experiment of his which bears on the supposed influence of the magnet. A lady told him that she could not endure a magnet being brought near her, and that it always had the most profound influence on her; and so it did *when she knew of its proximity;* but Braid, in order to test the nature of this influence, sat next to her on one occasion, for half-an-hour, with a powerful magnet concealed in his pocket, and, as he expected, found that no effect was produced.

DRUGS. Chambard places the anæsthetics chloroform, ether, and other similar drugs, amongst the agents for producing hypnosis. That, in some cases, a receptivity to suggestion occurs in the state produced by the action of drugs is undeniable; but the same may be said of certain abnormal forms of ordinary sleep, and it seems an unnecessary confusion of the subject to regard these analogous states as hypnotic.

LUYS' "MIROIR ROTATIF." This is an ingenious instrument, invented by Dr Luys of the Charity Hospital, Paris. It consists of two mirrors, rapidly revolving in opposite directions, and by gazing at this for a short time the sight becomes tired and dazzled, and hypnosis is easily produced.

Many advantages are claimed for this method,— that it saves the operator time and trouble, and is impersonal; that a number of people can be hypnotised at the same time by its means; and that it never fails.

I question whether the saving of time is really so great as might be imagined, for each subject must need the hypnotist's personal attention, whilst there are many other methods equally impersonal. Only fairly susceptible persons, and those who had been previously hypnotised, would, generally speaking, be influenced *en masse*, and these could be hypnotised as quickly by almost any other means.

I have, however, found it of great service in some cases, though, on the other hand, it has failed in instances where other methods have succeeded.

Dr Lloyd Tuckey and Dr Kingsbury both advise caution in the use of this rotating mirror; and though I have not personally seen any ill effects produced by it, I can well understand that in the case of nervous persons it might have a very disturbing effect.

THE NANCY METHOD. Hardly any hypnotist adheres rigidly to any one method. He finds that, where it is the brain that is most intimately concerned, the idiosyncrasies and character of each subject must be studied, and a method chosen which seems most likely to take effect.

In all these differences of details, however, there is one main principle now recognised by the whole body of scientific hypnotists, and this is the theory of suggestion.

The Abbé Faria, in 1814, is apparently the first who can be said to have made any advance towards the elucidation of this principle. Braid, in 1850, we have seen, by his insistence on the necessity of concentration and fixed attention, made great advances; but to Dr Liébault of Nancy belongs the honour of giving to the world a scientific exposition of the *rationale* of hypnotism. We have it from Liébault's own lips that he was first attracted to the subject by reading Braid's works, and he has constantly admitted that the Nancy system is indebted to Braid for its real genesis. In connection with Nancy must be mentioned Dr Bernheim, who has greatly developed and systematised the study of hypnotism.

The method in common use at Nancy is as follows:—

The patient is comfortably seated in an easy chair, with his back to the light, and the operator stands by his side, holding up two fingers of his own hand some few inches from the patient's eyes. The patient is told to look intently at these two fingers, and, as far as possible, to keep his mind a blank. As soon as the eyes begin to show symptoms of weariness, the hypnotist begins in a somewhat muffled and monotonous tone of voice to suggest sleep.

Sometimes the operator, without waiting for the symptoms to appear, will start at once telling the patient, "You are beginning to feel drowsy," "Your sight is getting dim," etc., etc., whilst in other cases he will wait till the eyes begin to blink somewhat, and then seek to increase the sleepiness by suggestions, which are made as the symptoms begin to develop themselves.

It is not to be supposed that in all cases precisely the same formula or details of treatment are followed; but the principle is the same. Thus this method of Nancy takes Braid's system of physically wearying the eyes, and combines with it a system of verbal suggestion, and this method is the one followed by the leading hypnotists.

As a matter of fact, there is no one plan which will succeed in all cases; some patients will be quite uninfluenced by one method of treatment, whilst they will be readily susceptible to another. Dr Moll says that he has succeeded in hypnotising by means of "passes," where fixed attention and simple suggestion both failed, and *vice versa*.

The dehypnotisation, or waking from hypnosis, is effected by suggestion, on the same principle on which the state is induced. Physical means, such as blowing on the eyes, may be used, but, in any case, I regard them only as aids to the suggestion, and their value depends entirely on the mental impression they produce.

Many means are recommended by various writers for waking the patient; fanning, sprinkling with water, loud calls and noises, etc. Just as the downward pass may hypnotise, so the upward pass (by reason of the mental suggestion it conveys) will serve to awaken; though some have claimed that the cool current of air caused by these passes is responsible for the awakening.

According to Pitres and others, there are certain parts of the body where stimulation has an awakening effect; to these they have given the name, "*zones hypno-férnatrices.*"

The forcible opening of the eyes will sometimes awaken the patient. I do not use, myself, any of these physical means, but rely solely on suggestion, though I frequently blow lightly on the eyes to ensure the suggestion taking immediate effect.

There is never the least difficulty or delay in ending the hypnosis, but, in all cases, the subject is brought back to the normal state instantaneously.

In the hands of an unskilful or ignorant operator the subject may pass from the waking state into a condition of apparent lethargy, and out of the hands of the experimenter, who is able neither to awaken nor to influence his subject. These misfortunes can never occur to the practised hypnotist; but many such cases are known, and the danger of these rash experiments in hypnotism cannot be too strongly insisted on.[1]

---

[1] A case is recorded by Dr Julius Solow (*New York Medical Journal*, March 14, 1891). A young man was hypnotised by a friend, at an evening party, for fun. The first attempt produced trembling throughout the whole body; a second trial was made with no better result; the third time, the subject was seized with violent trembling of the arms, and he began to shiver. He then fell on the floor, jumped up, became merry, laughed, joked, and sang; then violent convulsions set in, followed by loss of speech; catalepsy next supervened, and the whole body, except the arms, became rigid. For two days, convulsions, loss of speech, and catalepsy recurred very frequently, and the sight of anything bright excited the man to madness. Various sedatives were tried, and for ten days his condition was not much improved; but after this the severe symptoms began to give way to outbursts of alternate singing and lamenting, and after another period of twelve days, during which time his temperature went up to 103°, he recovered.

When once it is found that the patient does not awaken in obedience to the operator, *no further attempts to wake him should be made*, but an experienced hypnotist should be immediately sent for, or if one cannot be found, the subject should be allowed to sleep it off. In the one or two cases of the kind which have come under my notice, the harm done was almost entirely due to the ignorant and futile attempts made to arouse the patient.

The duration of the hypnotic sleep of the subject, if not awakened, is very variable. Some subjects will wake at the precise moment when the operator leaves them, the fact of his absence acting as a suggestion that they are no longer under his influence. Others will be awakened by an unexpected or loud noise. Some will be roused from the state by efforts made in it; thus, for instance, I have seen a subject awakened by laughing loudly in obedience to an hypnotic suggestion. If the sleep be light, subjects will often return to the natural state in a very short period; but, if it be deep, the sleep may continue for three or four hours. Dr Bernheim mentions one case in which the sleep lasted eighteen hours.

The condition after hypnosis is found to be perfectly normal. In the hands of an experienced hypnotist the subject never finds that he is suffering from any such things as "drowsiness" or "giddiness."

It is commonly supposed that those susceptible to hypnotism are comparatively few, or that, at any rate, they are not in a perfectly normal and sound condition of mind and body.

So far, however, from this being true, the reverse is the case.

It is practically impossible to hypnotise idiots. Voisin succeeded in hypnotising ten per cent. of his insane patients, but this he only accomplished after the expenditure of an enormous amount of time and patience. It is a commonplace idea that women are more susceptible than men, but it has been proved by experience that sex has little if any thing to do with the question.

As far as hysteria is concerned, it by no means predisposes to hypnotism; and, indeed, the whole class of ideas that persons susceptible to hypnotism are either hysterical, weak in mind, or weak in body, is contradicted by the experience of every hypnotist.

The subtle and intellectual mind is more easily hypnotised than the dull and the stupid; an healthy person more easily than an unhealthy one.

Nor does nationality materially affect the question.

The susceptibility of the subject is, of course, an important factor in the time taken to induce hypnosis.

By a skilful operator a large proportion will be hypnotised in times varying from fifty seconds to four minutes. Some cases present great difficulty, and several attempts are often necessary before success is attained.

Strangely enough, many of these refractory subjects, when once hypnotised, fall into deep stages of sleep. There are numerous instances, related by the best medical hypnotists, of patients hypnotised after sixty, seventy, and even a hundred previous failures; whilst it is reported of a lady, in whose case it was the only hope of cure, that she was finally hypnotised after no less than one hundred and ninety futile attempts.

Certain persons present apparently insuperable difficulties to the hypnotist, and these nearly all belong to that increasing class of "neurotics,"—who, in consequence of the rush and excitement of the present day, are overwrought, and suffer from what is termed "nervous prostration."[1]

The most difficult class of all is to be found in those of weak and vacillating temperament.

The most susceptible seem to be those in whom the emotional, animal, and intellectual qualities are best blended.

It must be remembered that the consent of the subject is absolutely necessary. It is impossible to hypnotise any person who is unwilling to undergo the operation.

As already stated, nationality apparently has little

---

[1] That extreme form, where the patient is unable to remain in any one position for more than a few moments, is particularly referred to.

effect on hypnotic susceptibility. The Dutch are not generally considered to be of an hysterical or excitable temperament, yet Dr Van Renterghem, in a report to the Medical Congress at Amsterdam on 178 cases, had only to chronicle 9 failures.

Dr Van Eeden says that he finds the proportion of the uninfluenced but little larger than that shown in the Nancy statistics.

In Sweden, Dr Wetterstrand found only 17 persons whom he could not hypnotise out of 718 patients.

Dr Tuckey tells me that ninety per cent., in his opinion, can be hypnotised, and my own average agrees with this.

Bernheim and Forel have both said that the opinion of hospital surgeons who cannot hypnotise at least eighty per cent. of their patients, is of no value.

Some physicians and surgeons, without any practical, and very little theoretical knowledge, have made one or two attempts at hypnotising persons, and, on failing, have rejected hypnotism as valueless. Such action is as foolish as it is unscientific. Even Professor Forel of Zürich found that, as his experience increased, his failures became less. In his first report he recorded eleven failures in forty-one cases; in his second report on fifty-eight cases, he had only failed in eleven instances; and in a third report on twenty-nine cases, there were only three failures.

Dr Liébault, so far back as 1880, had treated 1012 patients, out of which number he had only 27 whom he could not hypnotise. Here is his table—

RESULTS OF EXPERIMENTS IN 1012 PERSONS.[1]

Drowsiness	33
Light Sleep	100
Deep Sleep	460
Profound Sleep	230
Light Somnambulism	31
Deep Somnambulism	131
Unaffected	27
	1012

It is not, of course, pretended by any of these authorities that this success was attained in each case in the first sitting. Every hypnotist can tell of complete failure in several attempts, which he has only turned into success by continued perseverance. As a rule, however, under proper conditions, a patient, if he be hypnotisable at all, can be sent to sleep in six sittings.

One of the first practical difficulties of the hypnotist lies in securing the necessary mental attitude of the patient.[2] It is obvious that a person who sits down in an amused and sceptical mood, with an "hypnotise-me-if-you-can" expression on his face, is not likely to be easily influenced. By the

[1] See p. 146 for stages.
[2] Throughout this book, the word "patient" is used as the antonym of operator, *i.e.*, one operated upon.

ignorant and narrow-minded, whose philosophy coincides with their mental faculties, anything outside their own sphere is regarded *ipso facto* as unreliable.

My own experience, such as it is, has proved to me that susceptibility to hypnotism is the sign rather of a fine than of a poor intellect. With the educated and the refined my experiments have been uniformly more successful. On referring to my notes, I find that amongst members of the University of Oxford I have succeeded in hypnotising 96 per cent. of those I have tried.

The next important question is the depth of influence to which each may be subjected. Hardly any two cases of hypnosis can be said to present conditions precisely alike. The individuality of the person seems to be still existent under the deepest forms of hypnosis; but, for purposes of convenience and classification, the leading hypnotists have adopted various methods for determining the particular depth of influence at which the subject may be.

Edmund Gurney,[1] whose researches are valuable, though speculative, divided hypnosis into two stages—

1. The "alert" stage.
2. The "deep" stage.

Professor August Forel of Zürich names three states—

[1] *Vide* "Proceedings of the Psychical Research Society."

1. Drowsiness.
2. Inability to open the eyes. Obedience to suggestion.
3. Somnambulism. Loss of Memory.

Dr Lloyd Tuckey of London gives a very similar classification to Professor Forel's—

1. Light sleep.
2. Profound sleep.
3. Somnambulism.

Dr Liébault of Nancy has described six different stages—

1. Drowsiness.
2. Drowsiness. Suggestive catalepsy possible.
3. Light sleep. Automatic movements possible.
4. Deep sleep. The subject ceases to be, in relation with the outer world.
5. Light somnambulism. Memory, on waking, indistinct and hazy.
6. Deep somnambulism. Entire loss of memory on waking. All the phenomena of post-hypnotic suggestion possible.

Professor Bernheim, also of Nancy, suggests no less than nine divisions—

1. Drowsiness. Suggestions of local warmth are effective.
2. Drowsiness with inability to open the eyes.

3. Suggestive catalepsy slightly present.
4. Suggestive catalepsy more pronounced.
5. Suggestive contractures may be induced.
6. Automatic obedience.
7. Loss of memory on waking. Hallucinations not possible.
8. Loss of memory. Slight possibility of producing hallucinations, but not post-hypnotically.
9. Loss of memory. Hypnotic and post-hypnotic hallucinations possible.

All these attempts to properly classify the stages of hypnosis are valuable, and they are given here that the reader may form some idea of the variety of conditions represented by the word hypnosis. As a matter of fact, however, these divisions are not respected by the subjects. Phenomena are constantly found in one stage which are only supposed to belong to another and deeper one. As Dr Kingsbury says, patients vary as much in hypnosis as they do in their features, and do not respect any theoretic arrangements, but constantly overstep our scientific boundaries, and so render anything like mathematical exactitude out of the question.

M. Beaunis prepared an analysis of Liébault's figures, which is very interesting—

THE INDUCTION OF HYPNOSIS.

Age.	Somnambulism.	Profound Sleep.	Deep Sleep.	Light Sleep.	Drowsiness.	Unaffected.
Up to 7 years	26·5	4·3	13·0	52·1	4·3	·0
From 7 to 14 ,,	55·3	7·6	23·0	13·8	·0	·0
,, 14 to 21 ,,	25·2	5·7	44·8	5·7	8·0	10·3
,, 21 to 28 ,,	13·2	5·1	36·7	18·3	17·3	9·1
,, 28 to 35 ,,	22·6	5·9	34·5	17·8	13·0	5·9
,, 35 to 42 ,,	10·5	11·7	35·2	28·2	5·8	8·2
,, 42 to 49 ,,	21·6	4·7	29·2	22·6	9·4	12·2
,, 49 to 56 ,,	7·3	14·7	35·2	27·9	10·2	4·4
,, 56 to 63 ,,	7·3	8·6	37·6	18·8	13·0	14·4
Over 63 ,,	11·8	8·4	38·9	20·3	6·7	13·5

From this we see that the deeper stages are less frequently found in the old than in the young.

A peculiar mental condition is found in the lighter stages. The subjects say on awaking that they have not been asleep at all, and are quite positive that they have not been hypnotised; when challenged with the fact that they could not open their eyes, bend their arms, or perform any other forbidden movement, they reply that they could have done so if they had liked, but that they did not want to take the necessary trouble.

The discussion of these states would be incomplete without a reference to the Paris school. The schools of Nancy and of Paris are in conflict on almost every important point of the question. In such a *brochure* as this, it would be inexpedient to discuss these differences at any length, the more especially as the subject bristles with technicalities. A brief notice of the doctrines of Charcot and his followers must therefore suffice.

The chief controversy concerns the hypnotic state, and for the proper understanding of Charcot's theory I here append an extract from his writings:—

"1. *The Cataleptic State.*—This may be produced: (*a*) primarily, under the influence of an intense and unexpected noise, of a bright light presented to the gaze, or, again, in some subjects by the more or less prolonged fixing of the eyes on a given object; (*b*) consecutively to the lethargic state, when the eyes, which up to that moment had been closed, are exposed to the light by raising the eyelids. The subject thus rendered cataleptic is motionless and, as it were, fascinated. The eyes are open, the gaze is fixed, the eyelids do not quiver, the tears soon gather and flow down the cheeks. Often there is anæsthesia of the conjunctiva, and even of the cornea. The limbs and all parts of the body may retain the position in which they are placed for a considerable period, even when the attitude is one which it is difficult to maintain. The limbs appear to be extremely light when raised or displaced, and there is no *flexibilitas cerea*, nor yet what is termed the stiffness of a lay figure. The tendon reflex disappears. Neuro-muscular hyperexcitability is absent. There is complete insensibility to pain, but some senses retain their activity, at any rate in part —the muscular sense, and those of sight and hearing. This continuance of sensorial activity often enables the experimenter to influence the cataleptic subject in various ways, and to develop in him by means of suggestion automatic impulses, and also to produce hallucinations. When this is the case, the fixed attitudes artificially impressed on the limbs, or, in a more general way, on different parts of the body, give place to more or less complex movements, perfectly co-ordinated and in agreement with the nature of the hallucinations and of the impulses which have been produced. If left to himself, the subject soon falls back into the state in which he was placed at the moment when he was influenced by the suggestion.

"2. *The Lethargic State.*—This is displayed : (*a*) primarily, under the influence of a fixed gaze at some object placed within a certain distance of the eyes ; (*b*) in succession to the cataleptic state, simply by closing the eyelids, or by leading the subject into a perfectly dark place. At the moment when he falls into the lethargic state, the subject often emits a peculiar sound from the larynx, and at the same time a little foam gathers on the lips. He then becomes placid, as if plunged in deep sleep ; there is complete insensibility to pain in the skin, and in the mucous membrane in proximity with it. The organs of the senses sometimes, however, retain a certain amount of activity, but the various attempts which may be made to affect the subject by means of suggestion or intimidation are generally fruitless. The limbs are relaxed, flaccid and pendent, and when raised they fall back again as soon as they are left to themselves. The pupils are, on the other hand, contracted, the eyes are closed, or half-closed, and an almost incessant quivering of the eyelids may usually be observed. There is an exaggeration of the tendon reflex; neuro-muscular hyperexcitability is always present, although it varies in intensity. It may be general, extending to all the muscles of the animal system, the face, the trunk, and the limbs; and it may also be partial, only present for instance, in the upper limbs and not in the face. This phenomenon is displayed when mechanical excitement is applied to a nerve-trunk by means of pressure with a rod or quill; this causes the muscles supplied by this nerve to contract.

" The muscles themselves may be directly excited in the same way; somewhat intense and prolonged excitement of the muscles of the limbs, trunk, and neck produces contracture of the muscles in question; on the face, however, the contractions are transitory, and do not become established in a state of permanent contracture. Contracture may also be produced in the limbs by means of repeated percussion of the tendons. These contractures, whether produced by excitement of the nerves or muscles, or by percussion of the tendons, are rapidly relaxed by exciting the antagonist muscles. As it has been already said, the cataleptic state can be instantaneously developed in a subject plunged in lethargy, if while in a light room the upper eyelids are raised so as to expose the eyes.

"3. *The State of Artificial Somnambulism.*—This state may, in some subjects, be immediately produced by fixity of gaze, and also in other ways which it is not now necessary to enumerate. It may be produced at will in subjects who have first been thrown into a state of lethargy or catalepsy by exerting a simple pressure on the scalp, or by a slight friction. This state seems to correspond with what has been termed the magnetic sleep.

"It is difficult to analyse the very complex phenomena which are presented under this form. In the researches made at the Salpêtrière, many of them have been provisionally set aside. The chief aim has been to define, as far as possible, the characteristics which distinguish somnambulism from the lethargic and cataleptic states, and to demonstrate the relations which exist between it and the two latter states.

"The eyes are closed or half-closed; the eyelids generally quiver; when left to himself the subject seems to be asleep, but even in this case the limbs are not in such a pronounced state of relaxation as when we have to do with lethargy. Neuro-muscular hyperexcitability, as it has been defined above, does not exist; in other words, excitement of the nerves or of the muscles themselves, and percussion of the tendons, do not produce contracture. On the other hand, various methods, among others passing the hand lightly and repeatedly over the surface of a limb (mesmeric passes), or, again, breathing gently on the skin, cause the limb to become rigid, but in a way which differs from the contracture due to muscular hyperexcitability, since it cannot, like the latter, be relaxed by mechanical excitement of the antagonistic muscles; it also differs from cataleptic immobility in the resistance encountered in the region of the joints, when the attempt is made to give a change of attitude to the stiffened limb. To distinguish this state from cataleptic immobility, strictly so called, it is proposed to distinguish the rigidity peculiar to the somnambulist state by the name of *catalepsoid rigidity;* it might also be called *pseudo-cataleptic.*

"The skin is insensible to pain, but this is combined with hyperæsthesia of some forms of cutaneous sensibility, of the muscular sense, and of the special senses of sight, hearing, and smell. It is generally easy, by the employment of commands or suggestion, to induce the subject to perform very complex automatic actions. We may then observe what is strictly called artificial somnambulism.

"In the case of a subject in a state of somnambulism, a slight pressure on the cornea, made by applying the fingers to the eyelids, will change that state into a lethargy accompanied by neuro-muscular hyperexcitability; if, on the other hand, the eyes are kept open in a light room by raising their lids, the cataleptic state is not produced."[1]

It is seen at once that between these theories of Charcot and those of the Nancy school there is a very wide difference.

Dr Liébault, Prof. Bernheim, and in fact almost every authority in hypnotism, knows nothing of these phenomena produced *without* suggestion, with the exception of Charcot and his school, and one is inclined to think that having originally committed errors of observation due to the non-elimination of suggestion, the Salpêtrière school, in the endeavour to maintain their scientific reputation, have been too unwilling to modify opinions expressed when the study of the subject was less developed. Charcot has said, "At the very outset my studies dealt with hysterical women, and ever since I have always employed hysterical subjects."[2]

It seems plain, that, however valuable such studies may be from a specialist point of view, they can have little to do with the normal conditions of hypnotism; but so far from regarding these curious and abnormal forms as exceptional, the Salpêtrière school have jealously and bitterly attacked their Nancy opponents, terming their own production "*le grand hypnotisme*," in contrast to "*le petit hypnotisme*"

---

[1] Comptes rendus de l'Académie des Sciences.
[2] Magnetism and Hypnotism. *The Forum*, Jan. 1890.

—the name they have given to the state induced by the Nancy methods. When we have to deal with suggestive treatment the results will undoubtedly depend on what is expected by the operator; when, however, we have a state of "neuro-muscular hyper-excitability (not due to suggestions), etc., described as essential phenomena of the hypnotic condition, the question naturally arises, How is it that no other observers can find them? The answer is supplied by Messieurs Binet et Féré, prominent followers of Charcot, who admit that "results differing from those of Charcot will be obtained if the patients are subjected to a different *modus operandi*, if in other words *they do not receive the same hypnotic education*."[1]

It is to be deeply regretted that under the shadow of the famous Salpêtrière a position has been assumed, the effect of which has been to seriously retard the sober study and steady progress of hypnotism.[2]

The articles, which appeared in the *Times* at the beginning of 1893, entitled "The New Mesmerism," and the many articles, which have been written on the abuses of hypnotism in the Paris hospitals, have

---

[1] Op. cit., p. 100. The italics are mine.

[2] As I was correcting the proofs of this chapter, at Nancy, the news was brought to me of the death of Dr Charcot. It is, perhaps, well to say that, for some time, Dr Charcot had retired from any prominent advocacy of these views, and that his followers are responsible for many of the later developments.

dealt solely with the methods and experiments of the Paris school.

Dr Albert Moll, writing merely from the historical standpoint, has said :—" It is true that, as has already been mentioned, the study of hypnotism had been begun in various countries in connection with the work of Charcot. As, however, in consequence of the rather one-sided standpoint of these investigations, the different enquirers failed to find any lasting satisfaction, even the name of Charcot was powerless to give a general extension to the study of hypnotism. Only when the school of Nancy created a surer basis for hypnotism by a profounder psychological conception could people elsewhere begin to devote themselves on a larger scale to the study of it. In France itself, the importance of the Nancy investigators was more and more recognised. A. Voisin, Bérillon, and numerous other experimenters occupied themselves with the subject, and even those who had at first considered the experiments of Charcot to be of higher value, turned in large numbers to the school of Nancy"[1]; and Dr Tuckey, writing from the medical standpoint, says :—" Of the considerable number of medical men I have met who have attended Charcot's demonstrations, not one has looked upon hypnotism as more than a toy, and not one has adopted it for the treatment of disease; whereas all those I have met who have

[1] Op. cit., p. 16.

studied the subject at the *cliniques* at Nancy have been thoroughly convinced of the value of the treatment, and have adopted it into their practice."[1]

Much confusion has been caused by the oft-reported doings of the Paris school. Little is heard of the quieter and more scientific methods of Nancy, but the startling tales from the Parisian *cliniques* have not unnaturally filled the lay mind with distrust and suspicion, and it is now only consistent with scientific duty and a regard for facts to state that many of the experiments of the School of Paris are, unfortunately, unreliable and untrustworthy.

[1] Psycho-Therapeutics. London, 3rd ed. 1891, p. 53.

CHAPTER V.

THE PHENOMENA OF HYPNOSIS.

Natural characteristics—Various forms — Pulsation — Respiration—Effect of hypnosis on the eyes and mouth—Suggestive movements and inhibition of movement—Inability to contract, and antagonistic contracture of muscles—Movements made without and against the will—Means of Suggestion—Donatism—The muscular sense—Nature of the muscular contractures—Automatic Movements—Occasional state of Lethargy—Absolute catalepsy—Charcot and neuro-muscular hyperexcitability—Hypnotic anæsthesia—Dangers of chloroform, etc.—The psychological value of hypnotism—An examination of memory—Retention of ideas in hypnosis—The phenomena of memory in relation to hypnosis—Increase of memory by suggestion—False memory—Errors and loss of memory due to suggestion—Connection of motor disturbances with memory—Particular inhibition—Deprivation of perception—Deprivation of perception and conception—Post-hypnotism—Hallucinations and illusions—Value of post-hypnotism—Continuative suggestion—Deferred suggestion—Various kinds of suggestion — The post-hypnotic states — Their classification — Depth of hallucinations—Examples—Modifications of the pulse, temperature, respiration—Hallucinations, illusions, and increase of sight—Of hearing—Of taste—Of smell—Of touch—The sense of pressure—Hallucinations of colour—The muscular sense—Unilateral hypnosis—The mental condition of subject under hallucination—*Rapport*—Consciousness in hypnosis—The inhibition of the will—Reciprocal action of the will and the intellect—The illusion of resistance—The moral consciousness.

THE alterations of the ordinary functions of the body during hypnosis vary in their degree and number in accordance with the method of hypnotisation adopted, the depth of the hypnotic sleep, and the natural disposition of the subject. First are to be noted the phenomena of the state when no external suggestion is made, or influence exerted on the subject. Some are able to move with perfect ease and freedom : thus they will brush a fly off the face with the hand, or change their position when one posture becomes wearying. Others present all the appearances of being in an heavy sleep. Movements, if they be made at all, are very slow and languid. Between this ease of movement and the incapacity to move, there are many transitional stages. If the hypnosis be induced by means of the fixed gaze or by any method which requires some effort on the part of the subject, the pulsation and respiration are slightly increased.

The actual induction of the sleep is generally marked by a deep inspiration. During the sleep the breathing and the pulsation become slightly slower as a rule, but are marked by great firmness and regularity.[1]

The eyes and the mouth often show striking symtoms of the onset of hypnosis. The closing of the eyes is generally preceded by a marked quivering of the eyelids, and these vibrations are often maintained for some time after the eyes have closed.

It is not always necessary that the eyes should

---

[1] *Vide* elaborate tracings and tables in :—"Contributo sperimentale alla Fisiopsicologia dell' Ipnotismo." Morselli e Tanzi.

be closed for a person to be hypnotised, though this is generally the case, and in many instances to open the eyes would awaken the subject.

When the method of hypnotism by fascination is used, the eyes may remain open the whole time.

In the deepest hypnosis it is frequently found that the eyes are not quite closed, but that there is a slight opening left, through which the eyeball can be seen. Sometimes in hypnosis, as the eyes close, the eyeball turns upwards and remains in this position till the subject is awakened; at other times it is found that the eyeball returns to its natural position when the eyes are closed.

Perhaps a more subtle symptom is the strange effect which the induction of hypnosis produces on the delicate muscles of the mouth. I have never failed to observe this symptom, more or less marked, in every case whether the hypnosis induced be light or deep. Often the symptom is only recognisable by a slight compression of the lips; but frequently the contraction of the muscles is so obvious that the subject appears to be indulging in a grim kind of smile.

In any but the lightest stages of hypnosis all muscular movements can be prevented or induced by means of suggestion. Thus the statement, "You cannot open your mouth," or "You cannot bend your arm," is sufficient to prevent the action being performed.

The subject may be unable to make the movement because he cannot contract the proper muscles; whilst in other cases the suggestion causes a contracture of the antagonistic muscles, and thus the forbidden movement becomes impossible. The simple inability is frequently seen when the suggestion, "You cannot open your eyes," is made. Unable to contract the proper muscles, the subject attempts to open his eyes by elevating his eyebrows.

It is also possible to allow or prevent contraction for any one particular purpose. A subject, in response to the proper suggestion, will be able to say some definite word, but in all other respects will be absolutely dumb. He will be able to write, play the piano, sew; but quite unable to hold in his hand some given object.

As any muscular movement can be inhibited, so a movement can be induced either against or without the will of the subject. Thus the suggestion may be made that it is impossible for him to prevent his arm rising to a level with his shoulder; whether it is without or against the will has to be decided by the nature of the movement.

In the case of the movement made simply without any intentional act of the will, the arm will rise mechanically and automatically; but there is no evidence of resistance on the subject's part. On the other hand, the movements made against his will can generally be distinguished from the other class by the strong efforts and contractions made in the attempt to resist the will of the hypnotist.

By means of suggestion it is possible to compel the subject to cough, sneeze, laugh, weep, etc., etc.

Paralysis of a leg or a foot, an arm or an hand, can be induced in the same way. In the case of those subjects who are in a deep stage, and who are deprived of the volitional power of resistance, a series of movements will be performed by them if they be so directed.

It is important to note that while suggestion may be made, and usually is made, *verbally* to the subject, it is by no means necessary that words should be used. All that is requisite is that the subject should clearly understand what it is that is desired of him. The organs of sense and perception are all channels for the conveyance of any suggestion made to the subject.

It is found, for instance, that some action, on the part of the hypnotist, will tend to bring the suggestion more vividly before the mind of the patient.

This fact led many to suppose that the physical action of the operator had some intrinsic value; such is, however, not the case; its only value lies in its power of intensifying the impression which it is desired to create.

The professional magnetisers have been very fond of a particular method which is called, amongst other names, "imitation," "fascination," and "Donatism" (this last from Donato, who made great use of it). In this system, the operator fixes his eyes on the eyes of his subject, and after a short time the subject follows every movement made by the magnetist. If he lift an arm, the subject does the same; if he kneel, the subject kneels; and so on *ad infinitum.* Here fascination was the form of hypnosis induced. The same state can be obtained by opening the eyes of an hypnotised person, when the hypnotist, by gazing fixedly into his subject's eyes will be able to obtain these imitative movements. If the finger, or the mounted top of a walking-stick (see Fig. 1), be placed before the subject's eyes, he will follow the finger, or the stick, as the case may be; in all this it is clearly suggestion which is the basis of the phenomena. The subject will not perform any of these imitative actions, nor will he be "fascinated" by the stick, unless he fully understands that it is expected of him.

In very many ways, by a look or a movement, the hypnotist is often able to convey a suggestion to his subject which will be quite as potent as if made by means of speech (Fig. 2). This extreme susceptibility to suggestion is either not known or is overlooked by the ordinary public, and the professional hypnotisers often avail themselves of this common ignorance to deceive those who may attend their exhibitions.

FIG. 1.—*Fascination.*

There is a particular form of suggestion which acts, in the first place, on what has been termed the muscular sense. By this term is meant that faculty which tells us, without the necessity of looking, the position of our limbs. It causes a peculiar phenomenon in hypnosis. The arm of a subject under hypnosis is raised by the hypnotist, and then let go. Instead of falling to his side, the arm remains fixed in the position in which the hypnotist left it. In other cases, however, the subject will let his arm fall until the hypnotist gives the verbal suggestion that it shall remain rigid.

The important point to be noted is that, in each case, suggestion was the cause of this catalepsy; only in the former where the state was deeper and the subject in consequence more receptive of suggestion, it was sufficient to act on the muscular sense alone, whilst in the latter it was necessary to intensify the suggestion by speech. Of course, other means could be used for the suggestive intensification besides speech; if the arm were held in one position for some minutes by the hypnotist, or a pass were made along the arm, the intended suggestion would probably take effect.

It has been said (Moll) that these muscular phenomena of contraction must be distinguished from the suggestion which induces them, and certainly, the examination of any catalepsed limb is sufficient to show that in consequence of the suggestion there has been a striking physical change; but it is also claimed that in some cases the contraction is so great that a contrary suggestion will not suffice to counteract the effect of the first. I have observed numerous cases of the most rigid catalepsy, but this failure of the second suggestion is quite unknown to me; though, frequently, I have noticed a delay of a few seconds before the arm regains its proper elasticity. This, however, seems explained by the auto-suggestion which the contracted state of the muscle would naturally have on the mind of the subject.

If, for example, the subject be prevented from shutting his mouth, when the contrary suggestion be made, the mouth will shut with a snap, clearly showing that an effort was necessary to overcome the contracture.

While it may seem confusing to dissociate the effect from the cause, it is most important to note that the state of rigidity induced is, in no sense, imaginary or dependent upon the simple inability of the will to make the necessary effort, but that an actual tangible and physical contracture of the muscles does really take place.

Another common phenomenon of the state is that called by Liébault and Bernheim "automatic movement," and by Max Dessoir "continued movement." If the hypnotic's arms be rotated, or his hands set revolving round one another, they will continue

FIG. 2.—*Physical Suggestion of Fighting* (made by the placing of the hands in position).

to rotate or revolve. This again is due to an impression, made on the subject, by virtue of which the result is precisely the same as if a verbal suggestion had been made to him. Various and strange automatic movements will be continued by the subject, when they have been once started by the hypnotist, such for instance, as rising from his chair and then sitting down, working the head backwards and forwards, opening and shutting the mouth, etc., etc. The subject will even continue to walk, if he be properly started.

In some few cases an extremely lethargic state is found in which the subject is apparently almost impervious to suggestion, and appears to be in a heavy sleep. This condition is accompanied by great muscular relaxation; the head falls forward, and the body loses all its strength and rigidity, if left to himself the subject will often fall from the chair and sink on the floor in a huddled mass. It is said by some that these subjects are insensible to suggestion; but, in a considerable number of cases of this description, I have always obtained a certain degree of susceptibility, by adopting means calculated to strongly impress the subject with the suggestion; when this is gained, however, the response is often not decisive, and great languor still characterises all the movements.

The extent to which it is possible to obtain muscular contraction is clearly seen in the catalepsy of the entire body, when the whole of the voluntary muscles become absolutely rigid. In this condition, the body may be placed with the head on one chair and the feet on another, and will remain in a perfectly straight line between these two points. So complete is the rigidity that the body in this position will sustain an enormous weight without bending. I have seen a youth, by no means athletic or exceptionally strong, in this rigid state, sustain, without any apparent uneasiness and without any harmful result, a weight exceeding one-hundred-and-fifty pounds.

It must be said that, in addition to the various kinds of muscular contraction under hypnosis, which have been described, it has been claimed by Charcot and others that there are certain reflex actions to be found which do not appear in normal conditions.[1]

The stages of Charcot will be found in the previous chapter. It is sufficient here to notice that Charcot and his followers claim for what they term the state of lethargy (produced either by means of fixed attention, or from the "cataleptic" stage by closing the eyes), that there is present a

---

[1] Dr Moll (op. cit. p. 80) explains the terms "voluntary" and "reflex."

We understand by reflex action of the muscles that particular action which is induced by excitation of a sensory nerve, without the co-operation of the will. When, for example, an insect flies to the eye it closes; this closing is reflex, because it is involuntary. When on another occasion the eye is voluntarily closed, this is no reflex but a voluntary movement.

"neuro-muscular hyperexcitability," so that if any nerve be pressed, all the muscles governed by that nerve immediately contract; for instance, if the ulnar nerve be pressed, the fingers will contract.

Very few hypnotists are found who agree with Charcot in his classification of the hypnotic stages, and a large majority of the best authorities agree that these strange results were due to unconscious and unintentional suggestion on the part of the operator. Dr Moll has pointed this out clearly, when he says that since this source of error has been more carefully avoided the stages of Charcot are less and less frequently observed.

Wetterstrand never once found these stages, although he experimented on no less than 3,589 different subjects. The essence of the whole question is that, according to Charcot and his school, these muscular contractions ensue without any mental suggestion or impression being made on the subject. This is entirely contrary to the experiments and observations of almost all the hypnotists in every part of the world, and therefore for the establishment of such stages as facts a mass of irrefragable evidence is necessary; so far, however, from such evidence being in any way forthcoming, we have it on Charcot's own authority, that in twelve years only ten patients were found at the Salpêtrière in whom these stages could be produced. Whether these stages may occur in a few subjects is quite debateable, and I should be unwilling to state that they did not exist; but whether they do or do not exist, we may safely say that they in no way represent the normal phenomena of hypnotism, and may consequently be passed over without further consideration in an elementary handbook such as this.

Nearly every one is familiar, if only by repute, with the ordinary phenomena of the hypnotic state; motor impulses can be inhibited; deafness, dumbness, blindness, in many cases, can be caused; the special senses can be suppressed, so that the strongest ammonia can be held under the nostrils without the patient evincing any sign of discomfort. The proper suggestions being made, he will eat pepper and think it is sugar, or eat a tablet of soap with *gusto*, under the impression that it is a piece of cake. Indeed, almost every sense and organic function of the body may be affected. Anæsthesia is very often present, and can be increased by suggestion. It is quite impracticable for hypnotism ever to be used as a general anæsthetic, since, in this respect, its operation is so uncertain. Generally speaking, every one can be rendered insensible to pain by chloroform or ether, whilst only a small percentage of hypnotic subjects can be so deeply influenced as to place them in the same degree of insensibility. Dr Bernheim has plainly said that "hypnotism cannot be generally used as an anæsthetic in surgery; it cannot replace chloroform."[1]

There are, however, very many great advantages in the anæsthesia produced by hypnosis, which give it an exceptional value.

Hypnotism has never caused a single fatal result; whilst, in the hands of the most skilful operators, there is always present in the use of chloroform, ether, etc., the danger of a fatal issue.[2]

In many cases it is impossible to administer the usual anæsthetics, and, here, hypnotism may be invaluable to the surgeon. A case of this kind is reported, where an elaborate operation was successfully performed under hypnotism.[3]

The study of psychology received at first little help from hypnotism on account of the general neglect of its phenomena; the importance of a careful observation of all psychical states of hypnosis has, however, been gradually recognised.

This branch of the subject is deeply interesting to all who, in any way, study the human mind, and I therefore attempt to give an outline of the chief psychical conditions which are characteristic of hypnosis.

And, firstly, we take Memory, as being the necessary basis of all intellectual activity.

[1] *Suggestive Therapeutics*, p. 22, 2nd ed. London, 1890.
[2] *Vide British Medical Journal*, Jan. 3rd, 1891; also Jan. 10th, 1891. *Lancet*, Jan. 10th, 1891.
[3] *Vide British Medical Journal*, Nov. 15th, 1890.

Memory, according to Moll,[1] may be said to consist of three parts—firstly, the power of retaining ideas; secondly, the power of reproducing these ideas; and thirdly, the power of recognising the ideas and localising them correctly in the past.

Without express suggestion it does not appear that the capability of retaining ideas in hypnosis is materially increased. Beaunis has not been able to find any abnormal phenomena, nor has Max Dessoir arrived at a different result. The few experiments which I have made coincide with these. When, however, it is suggested that there shall be an increase of memory, the results are most striking. On this point it is often very difficult to avoid unconscious suggestion, since the mere repetition of any words or lines frequently acts as a suggestion that the subject is to remember them.

Whilst, however, the retention of ideas for a long time is not increased, I am inclined to think that, apart from suggestion, there is a greater capability for a short period, *i.e.*, the subject, in hypnosis, would remember more of a speech five minutes after its delivery than he would in the normal state.

To a subject quite ignorant of Greek, I repeated the sentence:—"Καὶ καταγόντες τὰ πλοῖα ἐπὶ τὴν γῆν, ἀφέντες ἅπαντα ἠκολούθησαν αὐτῷ," and I found that he could recite more, after one repetition during hypnosis, than after one repetition in the waking

[1] Op. cit., p. 123.

state. My experiments on the point, though they all tend to confirm this view, have not been sufficiently extensive to justify the categorical assertion that this temporary increase is a common characteristic of hypnosis.

The question whether the chain of memory, in ordinary life, is broken by hypnosis is not capable of any very definite answer.

In the lighter stages of hypnotism the memory is perfect; in the hypnosis the subject's memory of his normal state is active, and, on the ending of the hypnosis, he is able to describe all that occurred.

In deeper stages the memory is lost, unless, after awakening him, some hint be given to the subject, this will often serve to bring the whole chain of events to his recollection. Heidenhain instances the case of his brother to whom, under hypnosis, he said, "*Alles schweige jeder neige, ernsten Tönen nun sein Ohr.*" This sentence, his brother, on awakening, made many attempts to recollect, but entirely failed until Heidenhain mentioned the word "schweige." I have found a few cases of this sudden recollection upon a hint being given; generally, however, the memory is hazy, and often resolves itself into some such question as "Did you say anything about so and so?"

In the deepest states memory is entirely lost, the subject fails altogether to remember any event of the hypnotic sleep, and when anything, he may have done under hypnosis, is pointed out to him he manifests the greatest surprise.

A very important fact, to be noticed, is that, if the subject be hypnotised a second time, he will remember all the events of the previous hypnosis; and thus a deep hypnotic subject may be said to lead two distinct lives—the hypnotic, in which he remembers spontaneously all the suggestions which have been made and the events which have taken place during previous hypnoses; and the waking, in which he has no recollection or knowledge of these events.

There is no memory of acts done in the somnambulic state, because that association of centres and balancing of one mental function by another which constitute ideation, self-control, attention, volition, comparison, and memory are for the time being rendered inoperative. A patient under hypnotic influence may be compared to a complicated machine which is thrown out of gear, and yet can be so adjusted that some parts can be made to act independently of the others (Tuckey). Some persons remember all the hypnotic proceedings during their nightly sleep; it is not rare for the hypnotic dream to be repeated in natural sleep.

Another striking characteristic of deep hypnosis is that, not only will the events of previous hypnoses be remembered, but scenes of every-day life are remembered, and the most vivid recollection of things long forgotten can be induced. The acute memory thus evolved is seen in the following case :—

A girl in a state of somnambulism was in a room at the Salpêtrière, when Parrot, the physician to the refuge for *Enfants assistés*, entered. The subject was asked what was the stranger's name, and she replied to the surprise of all present, and without hesitation, "M. Parrot." On awaking she declared that she did not know him; but after looking at him for a long while, she finally said, "I think that he is a physician at the *Enfants assistés*." When about two years old she had been for some time in this refuge, and had long forgotten the physician, whom she recognised with difficulty, on waking, while she could, during somnambulism, give his name when ordered to do so.[1]

Another case, even more remarkable, is that of a woman of fifty, who was hypnotised, and who, to the hypnotist's great surprise, began to speak English, although no one present knew that she could understand a word of the language. During her waking state she did not know a single word of English, and it could be proved that, at any rate for twenty-five years, she had never spoken it. The only explanation possible, is, that when very young, she must have had some knowledge of the language.[2]

[1] Binet et Féré, op. cit., p. 136.
[2] Felkin. Hypnotism. London, 1890.

This dual memory (*i.e.* the memory of both the hypnotic and the normal life) has been termed "double consciousness."

The hypnotic memory is an element which the experimenter has to carefully guard against, lest he be led into many errors by neglecting the necessary precautions. If, for instance, the operator has been in the habit of connecting some particular touch or pass with the verbal suggestion of an act, he will find that, owing to the memory of the subject connecting the touch or pass with the verbal suggestion, he can dispense with speech, and rely solely on the touch for the production of the desired effect. This explains many of the tricks of the magnetisers, who have learnt, in the same way, to omit verbal suggestion and thus add to the mystery of their performances.

One frequently finds the subject interpreting some act of the hypnotist as a suggestion; on a first hypnosis I slightly raised the subject's hand, and then by suggestion made it rigid; in all hypnoses, since, it has been only necessary to elevate this hand to obtain the rigidity.

Moll[1] told a patient to raise the left leg; as he gave the command he involuntarily took hold of the patient's right hand. When, in a later hypnosis, he took hold of his right hand the patient immediately raised his left leg.

[1] Op. cit., p. 129.

Another instance of the hypnotic memory often occurs during hallucinations. Thus, if a subject imagine himself a general, he will lead the regiment into the field, incite his men to press forward, and will hear all the noise incident to a battle; if, after several other hallucinations, he find himself a child, some loud and unexpected noise during this imaginary childhood may serve to bring back the previous suggestion that he was a general, and he will promptly go through all his previous actions peculiar to this hallucination.

So far we have treated memory as we find it in the hypnotic state, naturally, and apart from the action of suggestion. With the introduction of suggestion we find some very important results. To the increase of memory, as occasionally a natural phenomenon of hypnosis, I have already referred in my experiments on the increase due to suggestion. I have not been able to obtain any really definite results, and this is due to the difficulty, already mentioned, of distinguishing between the heightened power belonging to the hypnosis itself, and that development caused by the precise suggestion. The only means of at all satisfactorily arriving at the degree of the suggestive memory is by first questioning the subject during hypnosis as to some fact of his life till his memory fails him, and then ascertaining whether he can throw any further light on the matter by a suggested increase of memory. Here, the results of my observations have, up to the present, been very confusing and difficult of verification, for, on the suggestion being made, the subject often proceeded to give a detailed account most gratifying, at first sight, to the experimenter. Unfortunately, in all the cases where verification or the reverse was possible, these details proved to be by no means correct, and I was forced to the conclusion that the subject, impressed by the suggestion that he could remember, forthwith gave an account consistent with the suggestion, but inconsistent with the facts. This spontaneous adaptation of mind, by no means to be confounded with simulation, is clearly seen in the phenomenon of *False Memory*. If it be suggested to a subject that he has been to America, he will give details of his visit, describe what he saw, name the boat on which he sailed, etc., etc. The details given will, naturally, correspond with the education and knowledge of the person. Thus all about America, that one subject could tell me, was the "White House," which he saw "in New York."

Another, however, though he had not been out of England, spoke with great accuracy of many of the American habits and institutions. Referring to the cosmopolitanism of New York, he said that one met every nationality under the sun in its streets; he described the political differences between the "Republican" and the "Democrat."

While my attempts at reviving the memory of past events by means of hypnotic suggestion have not been, up to the present, a success, I have been surprised myself at the extraordinary degree to which it is possible to increase the memory in the waking state by means of hypnotic suggestion.

Several Oxford undergraduates, reading for the University examinations, requested me to attempt to improve their memory by means of hypnotism. I anticipated that the result would be beneficial, but the effects in all the cases of weak memory which have come under my notice have been more than this. In one case a young fellow, æta 20, complained of the extreme difficulty which he found in remembering dates and the comparative positions of localities. In less than a week he was able to remember a whole page of dates after two or three readings, and this increase of faculty was permanent.

It may be said that such increase of faculty must have a prejudicial effect on the general health of the individual, much in the same way as the use of stimulants will, for a time, increase, but finally lower, the mental and physical powers. Such is, however, not the case if the operation be at all properly performed. The danger of a nervous lassitude and innumerable other dangers are all existent in the use of hypnotism by the unscrupulous or the unskilful. Properly handled, there is no method more entirely devoid of danger than hypnotism. This question will be referred to more fully later (see p. 221).

It is also possible to produce by means of suggestion either errors of memory or loss of memory. One of my subjects, in obedience to an impression of the former kind, not only maintained that the date of the Conquest was 1067, but commented on the general inaccuracy of historians in this matter; in another case the patient was induced by suggestion to forget, when writing to me, the number of the house in which I was residing; and I never received a letter from him correctly addressed; though, in obedience to the suggestion, he was quite able to remember the proper number when he called.

Loss of memory can be induced, and the recollection of any period of the subject's life may be completely destroyed. The subject can be made to forget his own name, his age, where he lives, or what is his occupation. According to Forel and to Franck it is possible to cause a subject to forget entirely a language he has learnt.

There are many delusions closely connected with the memory, in that they depend on this faculty for the induction; under this head may be classed the phenomena of False Memory already described.

If the subject be told, "You have just been running extremely fast; you ran half a mile as hard as you could go," he will, in consequence of the false recollection induced, gasp for breath and feel considerable fatigue.

Another suggestion may be made, "You have not had anything to eat to-day." On waking, he will not only tell you that he has had nothing, but will feel extremely hungry, and demand something to eat.

Many of the motor disturbances may be considered as related to loss of memory, since a movement is made impossible if the memory of it cannot be first called up (Moll).

This is the case with the paralysis for a special act, called by Binet et Féré "paralysies systematiques," and to which I have given the term "particular inhibition."

These terms refer to those cases in which the paralysis is not attended by total functional incapacity of any group of muscles interfered with; but where the function is interfered with for one particular purpose.

An hypnotised person may be deprived of the power of making himself understood by facial expression. In the same way any particular act, such as drawing, sewing, writing, singing, etc., can be prevented.

With reference to these particular inhibitions it is important to note that they range themselves in two distinct classes. The subject may be deprived of the perception, for instance, of a word or letter, and, in consequence, of the power to write it; the *idea*, however, of the particular word or letter he will, or will not, retain, according to the suggestion made.

If he retain the idea of the word or letter, he is quite conscious of his inability to utter or to write it; he is annoyed with himself on account of this inability, and will endeavour to avoid using it.

Thus, for instance, I suggested to a boy, whom I had hypnotised, that he would be unable to utter the word "Mary." On waking him the following dialogue ensued:—

Ego. Now, will you please repeat this sentence, "Mary had a little lamb"?

Subject. She had a little lamb.

E. No, I said "*Mary* had the little lamb."

S. She had a little lamb.

E. Please repeat the sentence as I quoted it.

S. (after a pause) "*Polly* had a little lamb."

E. Will you be so good as to say, "*Mary* had a little lamb"?

S. (indignantly) Well, I told you she had a little lamb.

After many evasions and excuses, I succeeded in finally getting him to admit that he could not pronounce the word "Mary."

The extreme acuteness of the subject in finding excuses for the non-performance of an action is often very marked. In the last experiment the

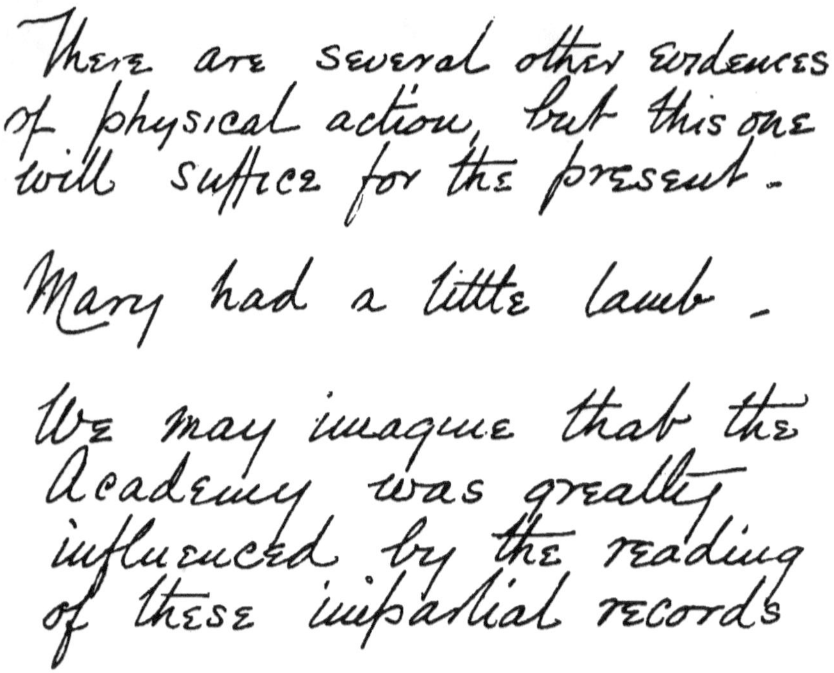

There are several other evidences of physical action, but this one will suffice for the present.

Mary had a little lamb.

We may imagine that the Academy was greatly influenced by the reading of these impartial records

FIG. 3.—*Normal Writing.*

(Reduced one-fourth.)

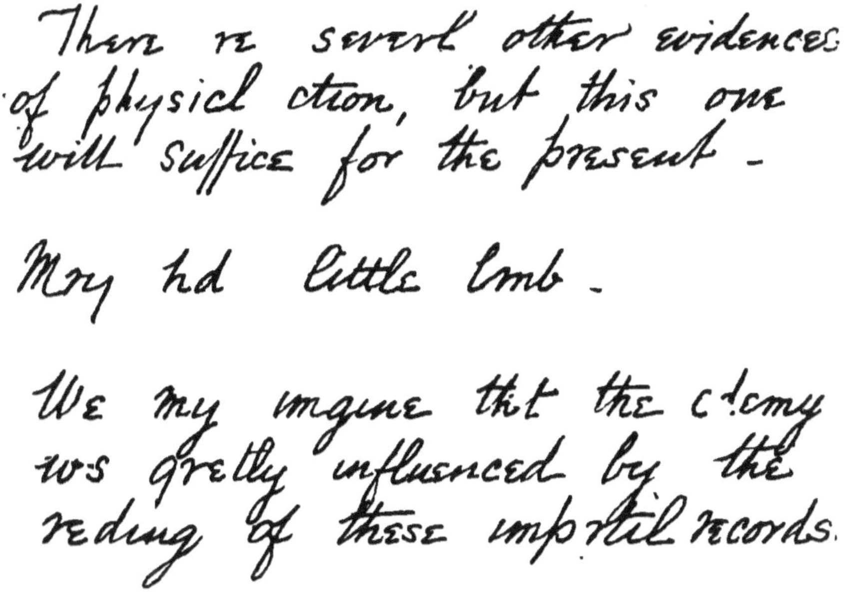

There re severl other evidences of physicl ction, but this one will suffice for the present —

Mry hd little lmb —

We my imgine tht the clemy ws gretly influenced by the reding of these imprtil records.

FIG. 4.—*The idea of "a" lost.*

(Reduced one-fourth.)

subject was a boy, ignorant and not of striking intelligence; nevertheless he endeavoured to avoid the word inhibited by using its nickname "Polly." When the subject is deprived of the *conception* of a letter, there is no manifestation of annoyance at his inability to write it; he, in fact, has entirely lost the idea, and, in writing, will consistently omit the letter. The illustration appended is a facsimile of what was written by an Oxford undergraduate, when both the power of writing and the idea of the letter "a" had been destroyed (see Figs. 3 and 4).

The reader will notice that where "a" occurs separately, a distinct space is left, and this fact is one of considerable psychological importance. I have often endeavoured in such experiments to obtain an explanation from the subject, of his reason for leaving these spaces; the only answer has been, however, that he does not know why; and he generally seeks to fill up the gap, when it is pointed out, by prolonging the "flourish" of the last word.

Almost any inability may be suggested. Thus I rendered a subject incapable of spelling correctly, with the result as shown in Fig. 5.

Reference has already been made to the suggestion made during hypnosis, but only acted on in the waking state; and to this, perhaps the most important branch of hypnotism, the name of "post-hypnotic suggestion" has been given.

By means of this form of suggestion, any hallucination or illusion [1] may be induced, any idea created. The suggestion made, the subject will become intoxicated (Fig. 6); he may see the most beautiful visions (Fig. 7), feel pain (Fig. 8), be impressed with joy (Fig. 9), or the reverse (Fig. 10).[2] It is not pretended that in all cases the experiments described in these pages could be performed with any hypnotic subject.

Not only does post-hypnotism afford the most striking experimental results, but it also gives to the physician an instrument by means of which he may cure with ease and facility many diseases and ailments incurable, or curable with great difficulty, by ordinary medical methods and after a long period.

Herein lies the exceptional value of hypnotism for psychological and medical purposes; herein also lies a great part of the danger of hypnotism.

---

[1] Sense delusions are divided into hallucinations and illusions. The first is the perception of an object where in reality there is nothing; the second is the false interpretation of an existing external object. If, for example, a book be taken for a cat, or a blow on the table for the firing of a cannon, we talk of an illusion, but if a cat be seen where there is nothing, we call it an hallucination. We have thus to do with an hallucination when an external object causes a perception by means of association. A chair in which a particular person has often sat, may by association call up an image of that person; this is an hallucination called up by an external object (Moll).

[2] It is not claimed that the illustrations appended are in any way proofs of the hypnosis, as the attitude and expression could, of course, be assumed without its aid. For the "expressions," however, a subject, whose features were peculiarly expressionless, was chosen, and in the waking state it was impossible to obtain any results so vivid.

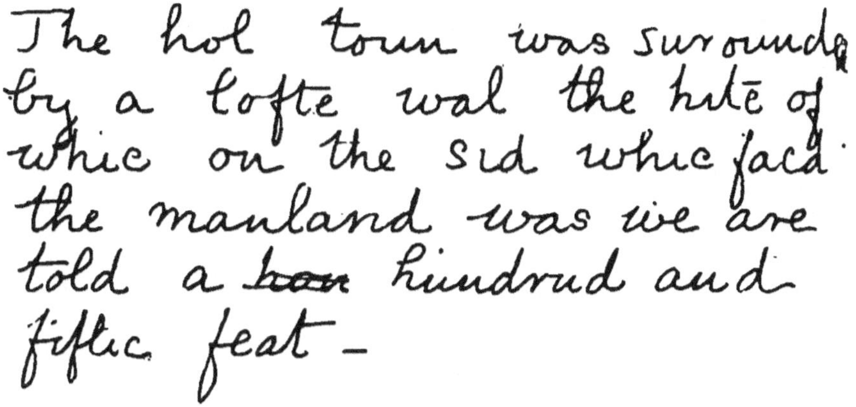

The hol toun was surounde by a lofte wal the hite of whic on the sid whic facd the maunland was we are told a ~~han~~ hundrud and fiftic feat –

FIG. 5.—*Absence of Ability to Spell.*

(For normal writing, see facsimile, page 196.)

(Reduced one-fourth.)

FIG. 6.—*Suggestion of Intoxication* (p. 184).

Any suggestion that takes effect in hypnosis will also take effect post-hypnotically. Suggestive paralysis has lasted for several days. Krafft-Ebing suggested to a patient that he should maintain a definite bodily temperature for a fixed time, and this suggestion was accurately fulfilled. In the same way, any movement or any delusion of the senses can be induced; dreams can be suggested, and sleep free from dreams.

A suggestion carried on from hypnosis into the normal state is called a continuative suggestion; as for instance when a subject is given toothache in the hypnotic state and is told that he will still suffer from it when he awakes.

A common but interesting experiment is the following. I make the suggestion, "You will count up to ten, and you will wake when you get to five." The result is not always the same; sometimes a subject will count up to five, then open his eyes and finish the counting in an automatic and mechanical manner; others will wake at five, and will not continue the counting.

Except for experimental purposes, however, the continuative form of suggestion is not often used, and the hypnotist generally relies on the suggestion to be carried out after waking.

It is not necessary to its success that the suggestion should take immediate effect. Let it be said to a subject, "When you come to see me this day fortnight, you will not be able to speak "; and on that day he is quite unable to utter a word.

There are innumerable forms of such deferred suggestion. It must be noted, however, that some forms will not always succeed with certain subjects. Thus, an hypnotic is told, at four o'clock, that, when the clock strikes five, he will find that he is at a concert, and will go to the piano and sing. Immediately the suggestion is given I wake him, and he will talk and conduct himself quite naturally, and will not have the least idea that any such suggestion has been made to him; only, as soon as the clock strikes five, up he will get, and seating himself at the piano will begin to sing.

In this case the precise time for the carrying out of the suggestion is fixed by an external sign, and these suggestions nearly always succeed. If, however, we do not name any such concrete sign, but rely on something less definite, such as a period of time, the results are more uncertain.

The suggestion is made to a subject that in an hour's time he will get up and dance; some will carry out this suggestion punctually; others will dance, but they will begin a quarter of an hour too soon, or (very rarely) a little late; with many the suggestion will altogether fail owing to its want of definiteness.

These "time" experiments are generally valueless when performed before a large number of spectators;

FIG. 7.—*An Heavenly Vision* (p. 184).

as the time approaches, the audience begin to give various indications of their expectation, and, as the precise time arrives, will look at the clock; this is quite sufficient to give the external sign often necessary to make the experiment a success, and, consequently, any result obtained is of no value.

Another means of deciding the moment for the execution of a post-hypnotic suggestion is the following :—I say to the subject, " When I get up and open the window, you will immediately become very angry." I wake him and we converse amicably till I open the window, when he at once begins to look seriously annoyed. I ask him what he is angry about, and he says, that " to open the window w is a ridiculous idea; did I not know that he objected to draughts," etc., etc.

The suggestion may be made more subtle if the subject be told to laugh when the hypnotist, for, say, the tenth time, taps his hand on the table.

As we talk together, I unconcernedly tap the table with my fingers; at the tenth tap the subject laughs. Frequently, though, the execution of the suggestion will not be so precise, but will happen a little before or after the exact moment.

By many subjects deferred suggestions will be carried out, though their execution be delayed for a long period. I suggested to a friend that, in eight weeks time, he should, in writing me, reverse my initials; during the intervening period I received many letters from him, all correctly addressed, but at the end of this time I received a letter addressed "Harry R. Vincent."

I hardly expected that this experiment would succeed—for, in the first place, there was no mention of any precise date, such, for instance, as July 20th, which would have materially added to the suggestive force, but only a period of eight weeks; and, in the second place, the suggestion was one peculiarly opposed to his knowledge and his habit.

It is frequently possible to obtain the fulfilment of post-hypnotic suggestions at extremely distant periods.

Sometimes these succeed when the suggestion is lacking in precision, as, for instance, "You will write me a letter, saying that you think I must be unwell, on the 40th day counting from to-day."

Success is more often obtained when the suggestion names some precise day. I said on July 10th to a subject, "You will come to me on September 20th and find me standing on my head." The suggestion was obeyed, and on September 20th he came, and laughing, asked, "since when had I become an acrobat."

The question naturally arises, "What is the precise condition of the subject during the action of the post-hypnotic suggestion?"

This is not capable of a very simple answer, because the state varies with the person hypnotised,

Fig. 8.—*Toothache* (p. 184).

and it is necessary to clearly understand the nature of these conditions before any explanation is possible. An example of each of these post-hypnotic states follows.

I. I say to A, who is hypnotised, "When you wake, as soon as I get up from my chair you will go to the clock and alter the hands till they stand at four o'clock." I wake him, and we talk together. There is not the least appearance of drowsiness or sleepiness. Suddenly I rise from my chair; immediately he turns to look at the clock and becomes, as it were, extremely absent-minded; in a moment, hardly paying any attention to what I am talking about, he goes to the clock and in a listless mechanical way alters its hands. I then suggest to him that he cannot see me, that he is deaf, etc., and all these suggestions he accepts. To destroy this state of suggestibility it is necessary to reawaken him. Here then we see three stages.

    α. Hypnosis.

    β. Waking state.

    γ. A condition in which he obeys the post-hypnotic, and is open to further suggestion.

Moll says that he is unable to distinguish the condition "γ" psychologically from a true hypnosis, and this seems perfectly sound. In these cases Delbœuf's proposition that to make a post-hypnotic impression is really to order a new hypnosis at a fixed moment, in which the suggestion will be carried out, is clearly confirmed.

II. I say to B, another person under hypnosis, "When you awake, directly I place my hand on the table, you will be unable to remember your name." After waking he talks to me and when I ask him his name, he tells me immediately; we go on talking, and I put my hand on the table; he is quite unable to give his name, though he seeks to excuse himself by saying that he has already told me a moment before. All the time, however, there is no listlessness or absent-mindedness, and he is not open to any further suggestions. If a day or two afterwards I place my hand on the table, it has no effect on his memory. Not only this, but he recollects perfectly the inability to remember his name on the previous occasion. Here we have no symptoms of true hypnosis.

III. I take another subject, C, and suggest to him that when he awakes if A speak to him he will make a grimace at him; if B speak to him he will put out his tongue.

A speaks to him, immediately he makes a grimace at him—each time A speaks C does the same thing. B speaks, and C puts out his tongue.

I ask him, "Why did you make that grimace just now?" He insists that he made no grimace.

FIG. 9—*Mirth* (p. 184).

"Why, then, did you put out your tongue?" "I did not put out my tongue," he replies, and nothing will induce him to admit that he performed either of these actions. He is quite unsusceptible to any other suggestions, and remembers our conversation; he only fails to recollect the suggested actions, and the remarks of A and B, with which they were connected.

IV. I suggest to D that directly he awakes he shall pace up and down the room twelve times; he does so, and during the time he is walking up and down the room, I tell him that the floor is very hot; he jumps off the floor and endeavours to spring ove the room in order to avoid burning his feet; I say that he is intoxicated, and he begins to roll about as a drunkard. Directly he has finished the twelfth turn up and down the room, I make a suggestion that he cannot hold out his hand, but he gives me his hand without any difficulty.

In this case, then, the subject is susceptible to suggestion so long as he is performing the act, but is quite independent directly he has completed it. This subject also remembers nothing either of the walking or of the sensation suggested.

V. The last condition I think it necessary to describe is a case of spontaneous waking. Thus I suggest to E that he will play the piano as soon as he wakes; he goes to the piano and begins playing. Suddenly I tell him that he has broken the instrument; he looks somewhat dazed for a moment, and then wakes up entirely.

He is able to recollect the playing of the piano; but his memory is not perfect. He tells me that it comes to his mind much as a dream does; in a few hours his memory of the act is still feebler, in a day or two it is quite absent.[1]

The important symptoms of these various stages seem to be the renewed susceptibility to suggestion and the loss of memory. On the question whether the state of renewed suggestibility is in reality a true hypnosis, many have made numerous experiments. Edmund Gurney, in particular, has contributed some valuable results on this branch of the subject.[2]

A striking experiment was once made by Forel. He said to a nurse, "Whenever you say 'Sir' to the assistant physician you will scratch your right temple with your right hand without noticing." The nurse talked rationally and clearly all the time, but she was quite unconscious that she was scratching her face, which she did whenever she used the word "Sir."

It will be seen, from the above examples, that the nature of the post-hypnotic state varies greatly, and

---

[1] In this classification of the states in post-hypnotism I have in great manner followed Moll. Op. cit., p. 144 *et seq.*

[2] *Vide* Proceedings of the Society for Psychical Research.

Fig. 10.—*Grief* (p. 184).

this variation is dependent on the individuality of the subject. The reader who wishes for more on this subject may refer with advantage to Liébault, Richet, Bernheim, Delbœuf, Gurney, Forel, Dumontpallier, Beaunis, Liégois, and others.

After this consideration of the various post-hypnotic stages, we are the better able to understand the phenomena of hypnosis and post-hypnosis which I now proceed to describe.

Hallucinations and Illusions. — Every one is familiar, at any rate by repute, with the ordinary delusions induced by the professional magnetisers for the purpose of their "entertainments," and it is unnecessary to describe them very fully. We find in profounder hallucinations many important clues to the psychological nature of the change wrought by hypnotism on the mind of the subject. Ch. Richet has recorded many of his observations, and I give one as typical of the deep-seated nature of the hallucinations.

Mme. A——, a respectable matron, underwent the following metamorphoses :—*As a peasant.* She rubbed her eyes and stretched herself : "What o'clock is it? Four in the morning!" She drags her feet as if wearing sabots. "I must get up and go to the stable. Now, La Rousse turn round!" She assumes to be milking a cow. "Leave me alone, Gros-Jean ; leave me alone, I say, and let me get on with my work." *As an actress.* Her face, so harsh and dissatisfied a moment before, assumes a smiling expression. "You see my skirt? My director insisted that it should be longer. In my opinion, the shorter the better; but these directors are always annoying. Do come and see me sometimes; I am always at home at three. You might pay me a visit, and bring a present with you." *As Archbishop of Paris.* Her face assumes a very serious expression, and she speaks slowly, in a voice sweet as honey: "I must finish writing my charge. Oh, it is you, M. le grand vicaire. What do you want? I did not wish to be disturbed. . . . Yes, this is New Year's Day, and I must go to the cathedral. . . . This is a very reverent crowd, is it not, M. le grand vicaire? There is still a sense of religion in the people, whatever happens. Let that child come near, that I may bless him." She presents an imaginary ring for the child to kiss, and throughout this scene she makes gestures of benediction to the right and left. "I have now another task in hand. I must go and pay my respects to the President of the Republic. M. le President, I give you my good wishes. The Church wishes you a long life; in spite of the cruel attacks made upon her, she knows that she has nothing to fear as long as a perfectly honest man is at the head of the Republic." She pauses, appears to listen, and says aside, "Yes, yes, only false promises!" Then aloud, "Now let us pray"; and she kneels down.[1]

[1] Revue Philosophique. March 1884.

In the same way a subject may be led to believe he is a dog, when he will go on all fours, bark, growl, and he will even attempt to bite freshcomers. As a pig, he will wander about the room, grunting and snorting, and indeed there is no end to the possible hallucinations and illusions which may be given to a subject. I append one or two of my own experiments which may seem worthy of notice. The subject of these experiments was an Oxford undergraduate of exceptional ability.

The first hallucination induced was that he was a little girl.

On waking, though his normal voice was somewhat deep, he spoke in a falsetto pitch and mii ed his words, whilst he sat in his chair, the type of meekness, with his hands in his lap. Some sentences were then dictated to him, with the result seen in the illustration (see Figs. 11 and 12). On another occasion, when under the same hallucination, he was asked to sign his name (Figs. 13 and 14). Another suggestion was made to him later, that on waking he would find himself intoxicated. He was with difficulty induced to write at all, as he strongly wished to be "put to bed"; after much persuasion, I succeeded in obtaining the specimen of caligraphy shown in the facsimile (Fig. 15).

On one occasion, when lecturing privately to a small audience, I told my subject that when he awoke he would find that he was Mr Vincent and that I was Mr A. On awaking he proceeded to discourse most eloquently, and "hypnotised" me as his subject. In the course of the lecture he had heard a few technical terms used; these he was not acquainted with, but, not to be outdone, he resorted to the most strange combinations of syllables, describing the nose as the "nasalium pimpolium."

Such facts as these might suggest to the reader a doubt as to whether the hypnosis was genuine; of this, however, there can be no doubt, and in all experiments which I record, the subjects have all been submitted to the most rigid tests, which no one could, for one moment, sustain unless in a deep hypnotic state.

In all hallucinations of personality the person hypnotised will always "live up" to the character as far as his knowledge will allow. It is quite possible to make the subject believe he is some inanimate object, such as a chair, a carpet, a piece of window glass, etc. I recently suggested to one of my subjects that he was a strawberry ice. He at once became flaccid, and, as the room was hot, began to "melt," till he finally sank to the ground in an amorphous mass.

Very often an illusion given will result in what is termed "auto-suggestion"; for instance, a person hypnotised early in the afternoon is awakened in five minutes with the idea that it is seven in the evening. He says he feels hungry and wants his dinner.

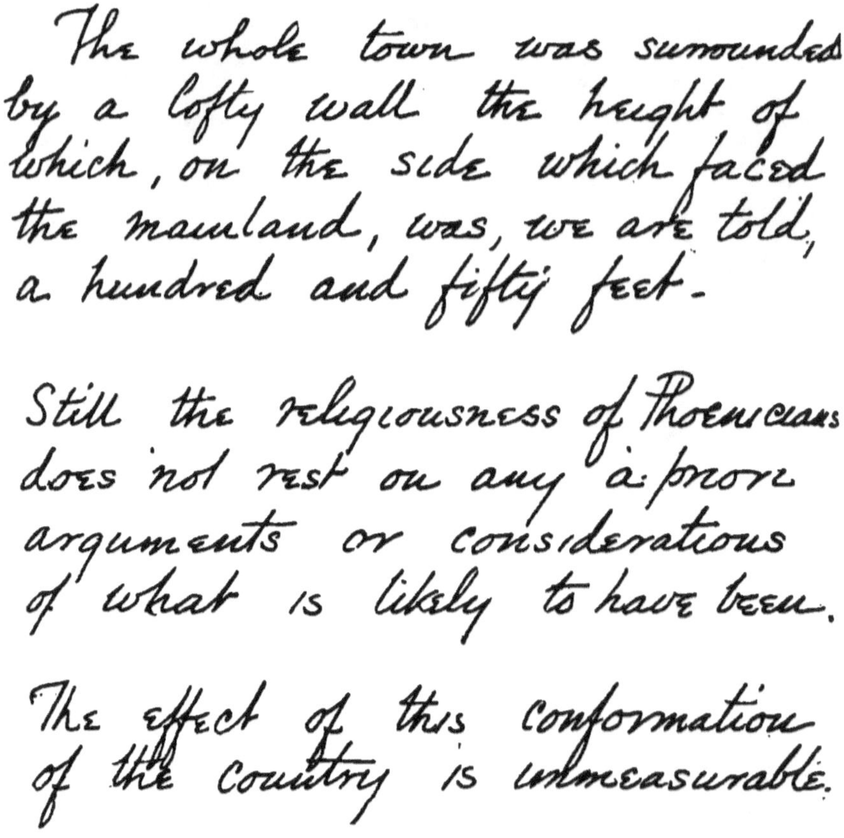

The whole town was surrounded by a lofty wall the height of which, on the side which faced the mainland, was, we are told, a hundred and fifty feet.

Still the religiousness of Phoenicians does not rest on any à priori arguments or considerations of what is likely to have been.

The effect of this conformation of the country is immeasurable.

FIG. 11.—*Normal Writing.*

(Reduced one-fourth.)

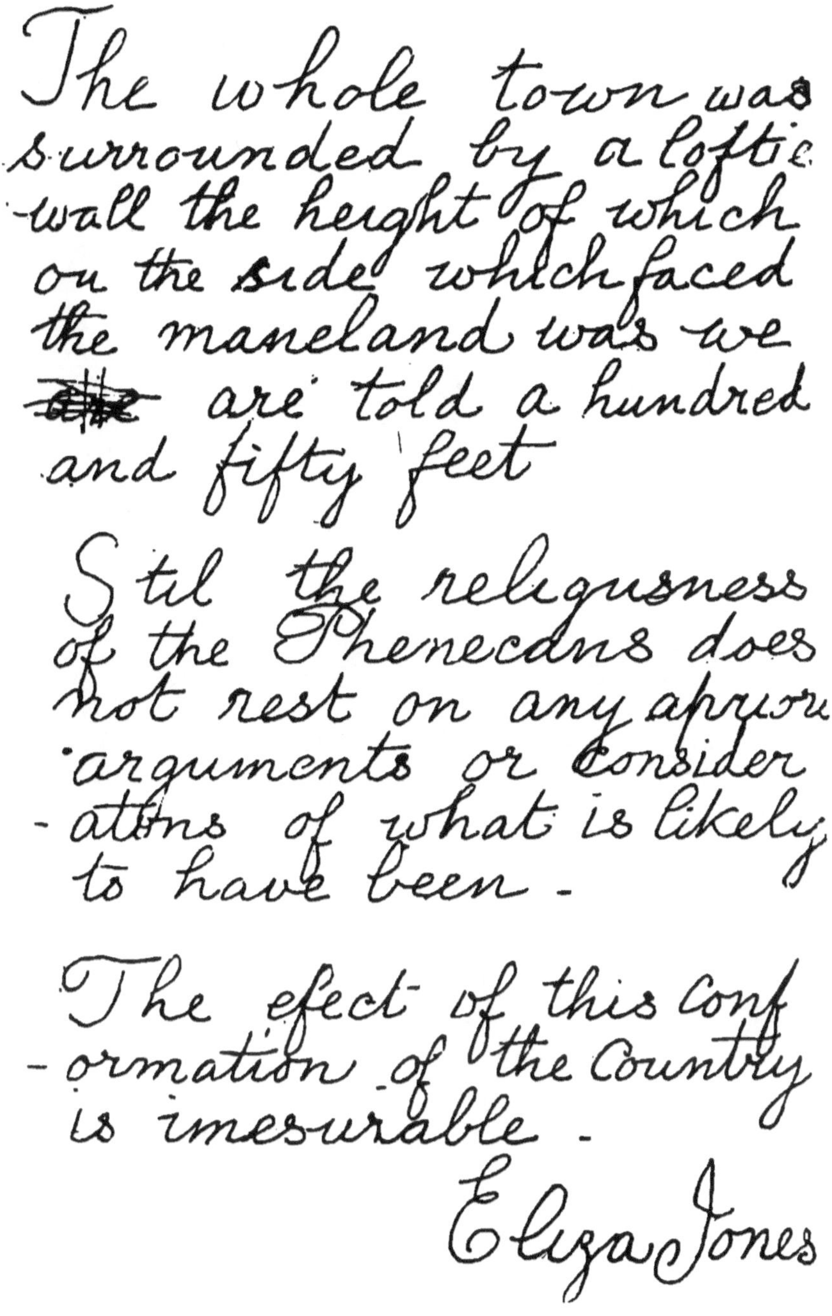

The whole town was surrounded by a loftie wall the height of which on the side which faced the maneland was we ~~the~~ are told a hundred and fifty feet

Stil the religusness of the Phenecans does not rest on any aprior arguments or consider- ations of what is likely to have been.

The efect of this conf- ormation of the Country is imesurable.

Eliza Jones

FIG. 12.—*Writing as a little Girl.*
(Reduced one-fourth.)

If it be suggested that the operator's hand is a pistol, on his clicking his finger, the subject will put up his hands to his ears and complain of the noise occasioned by the firing, the impression of which has been conveyed to his mind by the suggestion of his own intellect.

The following instance of a frequent phenomenon in post-hypnotic suggestion is notable. I suggested to a lady that when she awoke she should find that the floor was covered with tin-tacks and that she had no shoes on.

Immediately on waking, she huddled herself up in the chair and drew her feet off the floor. When asked the reason, she said there was "something sharp," and on being further pressed as to what it was, she said "pins"; this variation, slight in itself, is a potent illustration of the degree in which the whole brain is impressed by hypnotic suggestion; the word "tin-tack" was quite lost, and the intellect had taken to itself the idea or conception suggested by the hallucination. Binet et Féré, whose "general study of suggestion" is most scientific and scholarly, point out that hypnotic hallucination has always the appearance of a spontaneous symptom. On awaking, the subject obediently performs the act which he was ordered to do during the hypnotic sleep, but he does not remember who gave him the order, nor even that it was given at all. If asked why he is performing the act, he usually replies that he does not know, or that the idea has come into his head. He generally supposes it to be a spontaneous act, and sometimes he even invents reasons to explain his conduct. All this shows that the memory of the suggestion, so far as respects its utterance, is completely effaced.[1]

Some of the results which I am about to chronicle may seem so startling that I can quite understand these being received, by some, with a certain degree of suspicion; and indeed, in all such matters, the more scientific mind will naturally demand to, at any rate, see these phenomena before they yield their absolute credence; however, it is not my present duty to convince any one, but only to record the facts.

Anæsthesia. In all the deep states of hypnosis, complete anæsthesia can be produced. The most powerful electric currents can be administered without the patient evincing the least sign of discomfort. Teeth may be drawn and stopped, and any surgical operation performed without causing any pain to the subject.

The fact that this anæsthesia can be produced in all deep hypnoses, provides the experimenter with a ready means of demonstrating that there is no "acting" on the part of the subject.

The *pulse, respiration,* and *temperature* are capable of great modification by means of suggestion.

[1] Binet et Féré, op. cit., p. 209.

Eliza Jones

FIG. 13.—*Written afterwards, by request.*

Eliza Jones

FIG. 14.—*Signature as a little Girl.*

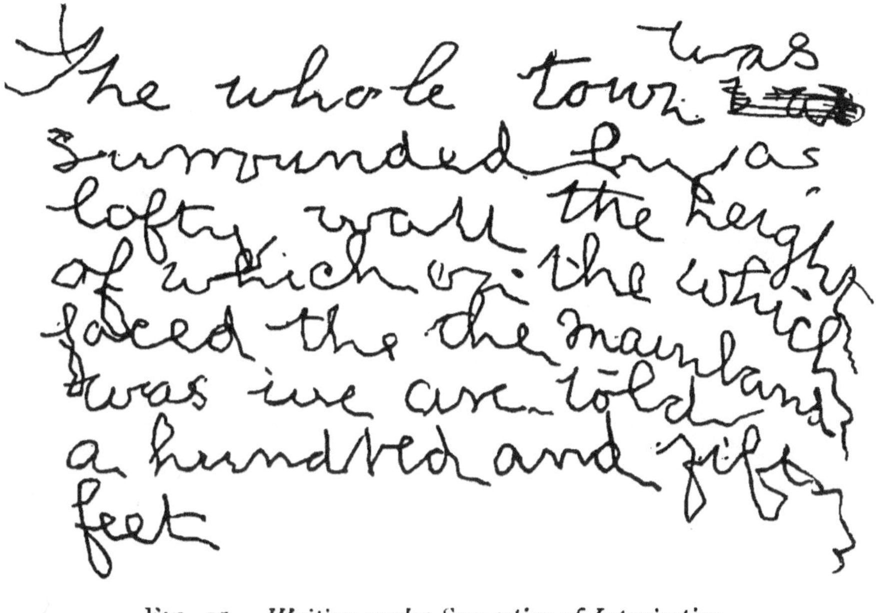

The whole town was surrounded by as lofty wall the height of which or the which faced the the mainland was we are told a hundred and fifty feet

FIG. 15.—*Writing under Suggestion of Intoxication.*

(Figs. 13, 14, and 15 reduced one-fourth.)

Krafft-Ebing suggested to a patient that he was in a bath, and produced "goose-skin" by this means.

Sight. The hallucinations and illusions of sight are extremely various and interesting. It may be suggested that some one in the room is another; the subject will accept the illusion that the hypnotist himself is some one else. Recently I suggested to an hypnotic that on waking he should find that I was X, mentioning a certain gentleman who was a mutual friend. Not only did he address me by the friend's name, but after a while, of his own initiative, began to discuss myself. The most complicated illusions can be successfully effected. I told an hypnotic that when he awoke he should find a friend opposite him to be the Bishop of Oxford; that in three minutes later, this same friend should be his college scout; then, after the expiration of a further three minutes, he was to find his own father sitting opposite; and finally, that the father should be changed into a collie dog. Not only were these illusions perfectly carried out by the subject, but the time was observed with great precision, though he did not look at his watch, and there was not a clock in the room. A person, by suggestion, may be rendered invisible to the subject. Binet et Féré relates an instance of this, every detail of which I have often confirmed by experiments.

We suggested to an hypnotised subject that when she awoke she would be unable to see F——, but that she would continue to hear his voice. When she awoke, F—— placed himself before her, but she did not look at him, and when he extended his hand, there was no corresponding gesture on her side. She remained quietly seated in the chair in which she had been sleeping, and we sat waiting beside her. After a while, the subject expressed surprise at no longer seeing F——, who had been in the laboratory, and she asked what had become of him. We replied, "He has gone out; you may return to your room." F—— placed himself before the door. The subject arose, said good morning, and went towards it. Just as she was about to lay hold of the handle, she knocked up against F——, whom she was unable to see. This unexpected shock made her start: she tried to go on again, but on encountering the same invisible and inexplicable resistance, she began to be afraid, and refused to go near the door.

We next took up an hat, and showed it to the subject. She saw it quite well, and touched it in order to satisfy herself that it was really there. We then placed it on F——'s head, and words cannot express the subject's surprise, since it appeared to her that the hat was suspended in the air. Her surprise was at its height when F—— took off the hat and saluted her with it several times; she saw the hat, without any support, describing curves in the air. She declared that it was *de la physique*, and supposed that the hat was suspended by a string; she even got upon a chair to try and touch this string, which she was unable to find. We then took a cloak and handed it to F——, who put it on. The subject looked at it fixedly with a bewildered air, since she saw it moving about and assuming the form of a person. "It is," she said, "like an hollow puppet." At our command the furniture was moved about and noisily rolled from one end of the room to the other—they were, in fact, displaced by the invisible F——; the tables and chairs were overturned, and then the chaos was succeeded by order. The different objects were replaced, the disjointed bones of a skull, which had been scattered on the floor, were joined together again; a purse opened of itself, and gold and silver coins fell from it.

We then induced the subject to sit down again, and we placed ourselves beside her chair, in order to subject her to experiments of a quieter nature. We shall see how she managed to explain certain facts, rendered inexplicable by her inability to see F——. That gentleman placed himself behind her, and while she was quietly conversing with us, he touched her nose, cheeks, forehead, or chin. Each time the subject put her hand to her face in a natural way, and without any appearance of alarm.

We asked why she put her hand to her face, and she replied that it itched, or was painful, and she therefore scratched it. Her tranquil assurance was extremely curious. We begged her to strike out violently into space, and at the moment she raised her arm it was arrested by F——. We asked what was the matter, and she replied that her arm was affected by cramp. She was, therefore, never at a loss; she invariably explained everything, however insufficient the explanation might be.[1]

The increase of the faculty of sight which can be produced is a striking phenomenon. I gave to my subject a blank piece of paper with the suggestion that he should find thereon a column of figures. He told me, in reply to my question, that he saw them. I then asked him to read them out to me, beginning from the top. The numbers which he read out are here given. My next request was for him to add them together and tell me the result, which he gave as 104. Asked to add the 1st, 4th, and 8th numbers (counting from the top) he replied, "35." The total of all the numbers consisting of two figures he gave as 65—an error of 2; he gave, however, the correct total (viz. 37) on being told to add together the numbers of one figure. Clearly, all this must have depended on the memory of the figures which he read out to me as seen by him on the blank sheet of paper.

8
6
10
14
9
4
18
13
5
12
3
2

[1] Binet et Féré, op. cit., p. 305.

On taking the paper away from him, I found it was impossible to obtain any correct results; he was unable to name any of the numbers beyond the first two. Thus the mental illusion was intimately connected with the surface of the paper, and resulted in an identification of the various marks and lines on the paper, more or less invisible to the ordinary eye, but rendered plain to the subject by reason of the increase of faculty.

With the object of ascertaining the length of time it was possible for the hallucination to remain in its entirety I allowed an interval of half an hour to elapse; at the end of this time the subject said he clearly saw the figures when he looked at the paper. In repeating them, he left out "9" and gave the number "18" as "8." Several other experiments were then proceeded with, and after an interval of two hours he failed to get at all near the proper order, though he still confined himself to the numbers, and persisted in guessing until I took the paper away.

That in all such hallucinations the increased faculty of sight plays an important part is evident from the following experiment:—

I take a piece of manuscript paper and suggest to him that it is a photograph. This sheet is then mingled with some fifty others of precisely the same shape, size, and form. The sheets are given to the subject, and he is told to find the photograph; he goes through the packet till he comes to the one on which it was suggested he should find a photograph. This he at once identifies.

When such facts as these are seen in hypnosis, the reader will easily understand how excusable were the theories of "clairvoyance," "prevision," etc., advanced by the early magnetists. The state, nevertheless, is a purely physiological one. If the piece of paper be turned round, the portrait is no longer seen; if it be turned upside down, the portrait is seen upside down also. All this, then, depends on the connection, held in the subject's mind, between the hallucination and the peculiar surface of the particular sheet of paper. These means of identification have been termed "points of recognition." Further still, if all these sheets of paper be photographed, and the prints be submitted to the subject, he will be able to identify the photographic copy as well as the original piece of paper.

Ch. Féré records an experiment devised by himself. "We place a blank card on a blank sheet of paper, and with a blunt pointer, which does not, however, touch the paper, we follow the outline of the card so as to suggest the idea of a black line. We ask the subject, on awaking, to fold the paper in accordance with these imaginary lines; he holds the paper as far from him as it was at the moment of suggestion, and he folds it so as to form a rectangle, which precisely covers the card."[1]

[1] Les hypnotiques hystériques considérées comme sujets d'éxperience, etc. Ch. Féré. Paris, 1883.

Binet et Féré have made many elaborate experiments showing still more clearly (although they do not altogether admit this) that in all hallucinations of sight some exterior object is seized on by the eye as the external basis of the delusion. If, when regarding external objects, a prism be placed before one eye the objects appear double, and one of the images presents a deviation of which the direction and the extent may be calculated. During the hypnotic sleep it is suggested to the subject that a profile portrait is on a table of dark wood before him. On his waking, a prism, without warning, is placed before one eye, and he is astonished to see two portraits; not only this, but the position of the false image, in these cases, is in conformity with optical laws.

Similarly, an opera-glass brings imaginary objects nearer, or, reversed, makes them appear farther off. It will not make the object appear more or less remote, unless it has been adapted to the subject's sight.

Lastly, it may be suggested that an object is placed on a given point of a table, and if a mirror be placed behind that point the patient immediately sees two objects.

Hearing. In obedience to the proper suggestion the subject will mistake the voice of some one unknown to him for that of a friend; or he will believe that, when a certain person in the room speaks, he barks like a dog, etc., etc. A simple hallucination can be induced by suggesting that, when all is silent, he shall hear the voice of a friend without being able to see him. One, thus impressed, maintained a disjointed conversation, asking questions himself and replying to imaginary questions.

The sense of hearing I have frequently known to be increased to an enormous extent by suggestion, under hypnosis.

A friend who could, in the normal state, only hear the ticking of a watch at a less distance than four feet, could, by hypnotic suggestion, hear it twelve feet away, and through a closed door.

Similarly, the slight clicking of a pair of microscopic forceps could be heard when the subject was at the extreme end of the room and the forceps were in the next room. On one occasion I got some dozen gentlemen to shout continuously the word "Tom"; amidst all this din, another was, in a low voice, to utter the same word. This latter gentleman stood behind all the rest; so great was the noise that, although I was standing next to him, I only knew when he had spoken the word by the movement of his lips. The subject, however, who could not see the speaker, immediately detected the sound and called out, as he had been instructed to do. This word was repeated thirteen times, at different intervals, varying from twenty seconds to three minutes, and in every instance the subject detected the voice instantaneously.

A still more subtle experiment was tried. As everyone knows, in a whisper all individuality of voice is apparently lost. If any one will turn his back to some friends and get them to softly whisper in turn, he will find it impossible to discover who is whispering, as the peculiar *timbre* of the voice seems absent.

Thirteen stood behind the subject, myself amongst the number, and we all, in turn, or out of turn, whispered the word "bother." The order was constantly varied, but it was impossible to deceive the subject, who, directly I whispered, recognised my voice.

Taste. The subject may be told that he is very fond of sugar sticks; if a candle be presented to him with the suggestion that it is a sugar stick, he will proceed to eat it with relish; in the same way, he may be told that some harmless substance, such as water, is nauseous, and he will evince symptoms of the greatest disgust on tasting it, and, in some cases, vomiting may ensue.

Under the hallucination of taste, poisons have been given to subjects with apparently no harmful results. A quantity of quinine has been administered to one hypnotised person which would have been sufficient to kill ten persons in the normal state.[1] 'Whether this be so or not, it is

[1] Dr Tuckey (op. cit., p. 169) says: "Several medical men who were present at a recent performance assure me that they saw

certain that the most deleterious and nauseous substances can be taken without the subject suffering from any apparent pain or discomfort. That such experiments eventually do no injury I am not inclined to believe; but, in any case, the absence of any immediate effects is most striking.

Smell. An experiment which I have frequently performed is the following :—A number of persons each take in their hands some small object, such as a penknife, a pencil case, a coin, etc. While the subject is still out of the room these articles are placed on the table, and the subject is brought into the room. He takes up the first object, smells it, and then smells the hands of the various persons till he comes to the owner of the object, when he leaves it in his or her hand, and so on, until he has settled the ownership of all the articles placed on the table.

Another evidence of this increase of faculty was given when I went, whilst the subject was out of the room, to some bookshelves and passed my fingers down the backs of several books. The subject, on returning into the room, smelled my two fingers, and going to the bookshelves pulled out the books which I had touched.

Many hallucinations of the sense of smell are

somnambulic subjects swallow as much as eighty grains of quinine in one dose, and that they watched for effects and found none. The same public performer made his unfortunate subjects drink large and almost poisonous quantities of paraffin oil, kerosine, and other nauseous compounds without producing any result."

possible. A foul odour can be suggested as sweet; and the subject will complain bitterly, under the proper impression, of the horrible smell given forth by a rose.

The next is an instance of auto-suggestion in which several senses, including smell, were involved. A subject's attention was drawn to a bottle of ammonia on the table before him; it was then removed, whilst the suggestion was made that it was still there. He saw the imaginary bottle of ammonia in the original position, but was quite unable to see, smell, or in any way perceive the real one. The bottle, containing the strongest ammonia, was placed, with the stopper taken out, immediately under his nose, and the subject felt nothing.

Touch. It is known that the sense of touch is not so delicate, but that on certain parts of the body (*e.g.*, the back), the two points of a pair of compasses are felt as one point. According to Berger, a person, in whom a distance of 18 degrees was necessary to produce a twofold sensation in the normal state, was able, under hypnosis, to distinguish the points at a distance of 3 degrees.

Sense of Pressure and Temperature. Very slight variations in temperature will be detected by subjects under hypnosis; and some curious results are obtainable by increasing the sense of *pressure* or weight.

Thus the subject is blindfolded, and a large horseshoe magnet is brought within about an inch of his hand. He describes it as "something smooth," "heavy," "feels like metal"; on a book being substituted, he describes it as "not so heavy," "something rough," etc., etc.

Hallucinations of *Colour* and *Colour Blindness* may be produced. Parinaud, the head of the ophthalmological laboratory at the Salpêtrière, has summed up these in a paper contributed to Binet et Féré's work "Animal Magnetism," and a portion of this I quote, though it must not be forgotten that these results are probably due to the hypnotic training which these authors have referred to.

> *"Hallucinations of colour may develop phenomena of chromatic contrast as readily as, and with even greater intensity, than the actual perception of colour.*

"If, for instance, a piece of paper divided by a line be presented to a hypnotised subject, and it be suggested to her that one half is red, the sensation of the complementary colour, green, occurs on the other half. If, after awaking, the sensation of red remain, so also does the sensation of green.

"In order to understand the meaning of this fact, I must refer to the following experiment, relating to chromatic contrast, which I communicated to the *Société de Biologie* in July 1882.

"A card which is half white and half green on one side, and wholly white on the other, is marked in the centre on both sides with a spot intended to fix the vision. For half a minute the eyes are fixed on the parti-coloured side, and then the card is turned and the eyes are fixed on the central spot of the white side. On the half which corresponds to the green half a red tint appears, which is merely the definitive after-image, and on the other half the complementary green tint is seen. The after-image of red has, therefore, developed by induction the sensation of green in the part of the retina which had only received the impression of white. This experiment, which may be varied in different ways, so as to establish the fact that we have to do with positive sensations, and not with any error of judgment, shows that every impression of colour leads to a more or less persistent modification of the nervous elements which produce the after-image, and that this modification causes, in the parts not affected, a modification in the opposite direction which develops the complementary sensation."[1]

[1] The controversy on this question is a very important one, but it is too elaborate to be dealt with here. The point is whether there be an affection of the apparatus of vision, the retina and the optic nerve, or whether the image be a subjective one awakened as a memory in the visual centre and evoked by the subject's intellect. The experiments of Parinaud would show that the alteration was of the former description, but Bernheim has made an elaborate series of experiments demonstrating that the image is a *psychical* and not a physical one. It does not pass by the peripheral apparatus of vision, has no objective reality, follows no optical laws, but is due to intellectual action. *Vide* Suggestive Therapeutics, 2nd ed., chapter vi.

Muscular Sense. If a subject be told he is holding a hat in his hands he will be unable to close them without using force, by reason of the resistance caused by the imaginary hat.

To find the amount of force required for the closing of the hands, I suggested that there was a roll of tissue paper between his hands and that he was to close them whether or not he spoilt the paper.

Here the difficulty was not great; when he held the imaginary hat it was greater, and on being told that he was holding a brick, he made the most strenuous efforts to bring his hands together, and he at last gave it up as impossible.

Unilateral Hypnosis. All the hallucinations we have previously discussed have affected the whole personality of the individual. It has been shown that by means of auto-suggestion, if a suggestion affecting the sight be made, the other senses all act in harmony with the sight. The phenomenon of unilateral hypnosis presents, however, an exception to this rule at once startling and convincing. I go to the right ear of my subject and say to him, "When you wake up you will find the sun is shining brightly, and that the weather is perfect." I go to his left ear and say, "When you wake up you will find it is raining hard, and that it is a dull miserable day." On waking, the result is very evident, and it is the more important as it is, I believe, almost impossible to be simulated, for the one side of the face will wear a smile, whilst the left side will present the appearance of annoyance.

I have also seen the subject, acting under such a suggestion, take an umbrella and hold it on the left side whilst he complains of the heat on the right.

It is often imagined that the subject when under an hallucination feels himself bound to carry out the will of the operator though he may himself recognise the absurdity of the suggestion. Of course, there are cases where the suggestion is only partially received; but generally the subject is quite unconscious of the fact that he is acting under the influence of an hypnotic suggestion.

I put his college cap in the lap of a subject, and told him that when he awoke he would find it was a little fox terrier. Previous to hypnotising him, I had said that I was going to give him an hallucination, and wished him to remember, on waking, that whatever he saw was due to a suggestion I had given him in hypnosis. The look of incredulous surprise, with which he regarded me when I said that it was not a dog he had in his lap, but a college cap, was more than sufficient to show how completely the warning had failed to overthrow the suggestion.

"Not a dog," said he; "pray, then, what do you call it?" And on my taking up the tassel of the cap, he was angry with me for "pulling the dog's tail." I then asked him if he did not remember my warning before he was hypnotised, and assured him that it was a cap he had in his lap, and that he mistook it for a dog by means of the hypnotic suggestion I had given to him. He looked at me with a puzzled expression for some moments, and finally laughed, saying, "You must have been hypnotised yourself, I think."

I must now refer to a frequent and important symptom of hypnosis which is called *rapport*.

This is present in all the deep stages of hypnosis, and is seen by the fact that the subject will only pay attention to what the hypnotist says. To anything which the onlookers may say or do he is quite oblivious. If this condition of *rapport* be not present, spontaneously, it may be evoked by means of suggestion. In the same way, the subject can be put into *rapport* with anyone else on the proper suggestion being made by the hypnotist. A great deal has been written on the subject of this connection between the subject and hypnotist; many of the theories advanced to explain the phenomenon seem somewhat wild and unnecessary. Thus, Dr Moll, in discussing the analogies of *rapport* in the waking state, writes—

"We see this every day in ordinary life, and particularly in love affairs. It happens often that one person is attracted by another and repelled by a third, without being able to discover his reasons for it. Reason often points out the perversity of his inclination; and yet he cannot overcome the strong mental influence which attracts him. *De gustibus non est disputandum;* it is useless to argue about our tastes, because they are not guided by reason, but by certain undefined agencies. To call these feelings sympathies and antipathies explains nothing."[1]

The hypnotic rapport seems to me capable of a simpler explanation. The subject goes to sleep with the hypnotist watching him; no one else touches him or speaks to him, and the suggestion at once creeps into the subject's mind that he is in touch with the operator alone.

It is evident from the discussion of the many hypnotic phenomena, which, as we have seen, depend largely for their production upon the action of the intellect and the memory, that with regard to hypnosis it would be altogether misleading and false to speak of "unconsciousness," understanding by this term the psychological meaning—*i.e.*, a state in which no psychical process takes place.

It is equally clear, however, that though it be inaccurate to speak of loss of consciousness in hypnosis, we have nevertheless to do with a singular and abnormal form of consciousness.

The etiological theories advanced by the various authorities on the subject are extremely numerous, though now there seems to be a nearer approach

[1] Op. cit., p. 62.

to unanimity than was the case a few years ago.

The main characteristic of hypnosis seems to be the temporary inhibition of the volitional power of the brain. This inhibition varies in its degree and nature with every subject, and no two hypnotised persons present precisely the same symptoms—an evidence that even in the deepest hypnoses the individuality of the subject is not destroyed. Let us take an example of volitional action in the normal life. If a person be told to raise his arm, this order is conveyed first to the centre of hearing and thence to the highest centres, which consider the circumstances and reasonableness of such action; if those centres of emotion and reflection favour the execution of the order, then the will sends an impulse to the motor centres, and the arm is raised.

If the order be given in an imperative tone to one accustomed to obey the voice of authority the action will be carried out automatically; the command will be referred directly from the auditory centre to the muscles of the arm (Tuckey).

In such a case, where the order is followed by its automatic action, the two stand in the relation of cause and effect. Tuckey quotes on this point the story of an old soldier who, while carrying home his Sunday dinner, was hailed by a practical joker, who called "Attention!" His arms immediately fell into the required position, and the dinner rolled in the gutter.

If the reasoning and debating centres, generally speaking, need to act before the volitional centre will send the necessary motor impulse, so the will may have a reciprocal effect on the intellect; and these two functions of the brain maintain, between themselves, an harmony very subtle, but very perfect. Thus, by means of expectant attention and the concentration of the faculties which are present whenever the hypnosis is being induced, we obtain a suspension at first, on the part of the subject voluntary and intentional, of the reasoning powers; and then, by means of suggestions, this suspension is increased and intensified till the brain assumes a state of high perceptive power, and of largely increased *receptivity*.

In this manner, as exemplified to a certain degree in the case of the soldier, the whole nerve force of the subject is, so to speak, at the disposal of the hypnotist, who, without hindrance or delay from the reasoning or volitional centres, may direct all its force to any function of the body. That the inhibition of the intellect and will plays an important part in the state of hypnosis is seen perhaps more clearly by a reference to the light hypnotic states, where these two functions have only been slightly affected.

It is quite a common experience for the hypnotist

to be told by a subject who has only been slightly influenced that he has not really been hypnotised at all. He remembers perfectly all that took place under the hypnosis, and explains his inability to open his eyes or part his hands by saying he could have done so if he wished, only he did not want to bother about trying. This is termed the "illusion of resistance."

Another subject may be in such a light state that it is impossible to prevent any muscular action; nevertheless, toothache or any similar pain may be taken away with the greatest ease.

The fact that, on waking, subjects find the pain completely gone, convinces them of what they would otherwise have stoutly denied, viz., that hypnosis has been induced.

In such light states, if the patient has not been suffering, previous to his hypnosis, from some ailment, it is sometimes quite impossible to persuade him that he has been in the least degree hypnotised.

Perhaps the most curious instance of this tendency is seen in the following case:—A friend, whom I had hypnotised several times previously, complained of feeling very ill and depressed—a complaint that was borne out by his appearance. I hypnotised him, and he fell, in about a minute, into his usual state of light sleep. When I had finished the operation and was going to wake him, he suddenly said, in a very measured and listless manner, indicative of the fact that he was still under the influence, "You know, Vincent, I'm not hypnotised; you couldn't prevent me doing anything." I immediately awoke him, and he was profoundly astonished to find that so far from being ill and depressed, he felt well and happy. Had it not been for the fact that he was previously suffering from depression, nothing would have convinced him that he had been hypnotised.

Richet has described much the same phenomenon:—

"One of my friends, who was drowsy but not quite asleep, carefully studied this phenomenon of incapacity, combined with the illusion of capacity. When I prescribed a movement, he always performed it, even although he had, before he was magnetised, been determined to resist. He found this hard to understand when he awoke, and said that he certainly could have resisted, only he did not wish to do so. Sometimes he was inclined to believe that he was simulating. "When I am asleep," he said, "I feign automatism, although I believe that I might act otherwise. I begin with the firm determination not to simulate, but as soon as I am asleep it seems that, in spite of myself, simulation begins."

A still more important phenomenon of hypnosis is the presence of a latent moral consciousness which will prevent the subject saying anything or performing any act repulsive to him. I had no difficulty in persuading a rigid total abstainer that a glass of water in front of him was a glass of wine; but, when I suggested that he would be bound to drink the imaginary wine, he forthwith awoke.

I put a steel dagger into the hand of a subject, with the suggestion that, on awaking, he should stab me. The order was not obeyed.

The possibilities of criminal suggestion will be considered in another chapter; it is sufficient here to state that, in general, any such suggestion will either end the hypnosis forthwith, or be disobeyed.

In these few pages I have endeavoured to give a brief account of the chief phenomena which are commonly to be noticed in hypnosis; many interesting questions have been left untouched, since they would have led me too far from my original purpose, and would have involved much tentative discussion; but I trust this chapter may be sufficient to give the reader a fairly complete idea of the main phenomena.

CHAPTER VI.

THE DANGERS OF HYPNOTISM.

Various objections to hypnotism—Superstition—Bigotry—Harvey—Attacks made on hypnotism—Dr Norman Kerr—Sir Andrew Clark—Dr W. B. Richardson—The violence of their language—The absence of evidence—Some misconceptions concerning hypnotism—The testimony of Bernheim, Liébault, and others—The danger of the subject not awaking—Ignorant hypnotisation—Consent of subject always necessary for induction of hypnosis—Influence at a distance—The real dangers—The Gouffé trial—Criminal assaults—Experiments of Liégois—Of Gilles de la Tourette—Luys—Laboratory experiments—Bernheim's rules—The necessity of legislative restrictions.

MANY objections are urged against the use of hypnotism, and it is my purpose in this chapter to eliminate the real from the unreal, and to try and show where the real dangers of hypnotism rest. Firstly, there are objections which are so silly that, were it not for the number of their supporters, it would be unnecessary to mention them.

Dr Kingsbury says that "at the end of the nineteenth century it seems hardly credible that a solitary individual could be found to believe that hypnotism is in some way a kind of *black art.*" Nevertheless, in not a few cases I have found persons bigoted enough to suggest that there was a *Satanic* element in it. I suppose every hypnotist is familiar with that uplifting of the eyebrows and reproving shake of the head, which are meant to convey that the whole thing is, to say the least, "questionable."

An estimable and cultured lady of my acquaintance has such an horror of hypnotism, and all connected with it, that I believe she expects to hear one day that I am "possessed" of the devil of hypnotism! To argue with such people would, of course, be ridiculous. One might as well try and carry on an interesting conversation with the garden gate. This kind of opposition, however, almost every modern discovery has had to meet, and the strange thing is that all the new scholarship and culture of our era do not seem to have much influence on it. When the Jesuits in 1649 introduced Peruvian bark into Europe, its use was prohibited on the ground that its cures were too rapid, and that it possessed no virtue but what it derived from a compact made by the Indians with the devil!

The introduction of vaccination was the signal for the outburst of almost every form of religious fanaticism. "Hellish," "devilish," "Antichrist," were some of the names applied to that which has practically freed this country from the real smallpox.

Kingsbury quotes a celebrated preacher of his time, who, preaching in Liverpool in 1844, said, "I have seen nothing of it, nor do I think it right to tempt God by going to see it. I have not faith to go in the name of the Lord Jesus, and to command the devil to depart."

This is bigotry *par excellence*, and the same spirit exists to-day, not only with regard to hypnotism, but with regard to every advance made by science. The young lady thinks it is "wrong," and the old man thinks "it ought to be put a stop to."

Hume, in his "History of England," has told us that no physician in Europe who had reached forty years of age ever to the end of his life adopted Harvey's doctrine of the circulation of the blood.

Dr Norman Kerr, Sir Andrew Clark, Dr W. B. Richardson, and others, have attacked hypnotism with such vehemence that it seems as if the English language would need a fresh supply of adjectives were these attacks at all persistent.

The curious fact is, however, that none of these gentlemen produce evidence of their extraordinary statements. Sir Andrew Clark rejects the evidence of some of the greatest authorities as prejudiced, and then proceeds to discourse on his own "experience," without giving any corroboration, in the shape of fact, of his unwarrantable statements.

The nature of the evidence that can be brought against hypnotism is clearly shown by its most virulent opponent, Dr Norman Kerr, who, according to his own account, after thirty years' observation of hypnotism, knew at least one case in which, after apparent benefit from hypnotic treatment, mental instability passed into insanity. That in *one case* a man mentally unstable finally became insane does not seem a very crushing indictment; and even the learned doctor himself does not tell us that this final state was in consequence of, but only subsequent to, hypnotism.

There are certain popular misconceptions with regard to hypnotism which greatly prejudice the public mind against its use, and which have only to be dissolved for it to obtain a fairer hearing.

Thus, for instance, it is often said that hypnotism results in the weakening of the subject's intelligence and brain power.

To this idea, which is nothing more than a superstition, must be opposed the testimony of every hypnotist who has practised largely. The precise statements of these numerous authorities might be quoted, but two will suffice. After Dr Bernheim had induced hypnosis over 10,000 times, he said, " I have never seen any harm produced by sleep induced according to our method"; and Dr Liébault, after thirty years' continuous practice of hypnotism, says that he cannot recall a single occasion on which he regrets having adopted treatment by hypnotism. I need hardly say that in the hands of the ignorant hypnotism may be the cause of untold dangers; but this is its abuse and not its use.

Another common idea is that the subject, once

hypnotised, may not waken. Any properly qualified operator would of course laugh at the suggestion of such a possibility. In no single case has there been the least difficulty in waking the subject where the state has been induced by a competent person; in fact, the transition from the hypnotic to the waking state is, at most, a matter of a few seconds, and is practically instantaneous. Not only is there no difficulty in awaking the subject, but he returns to the normal state in a perfectly natural condition, free from all drowsiness or weariness.

The origin of these ideas lies in ignorant amateur hypnotisation. I have had several cases brought before my notice, where the most serious symptoms were present after awaking. Quite recently a case came before me of an Oxford undergraduate who was hypnotised by an amateur one Wednesday. During the rest of the week he was so drowsy that on several occasions he could not keep awake. One afternoon while having tea with some friends he fell fast asleep. On the following Sunday he came to me to see if these effects could be removed. As no serious harm had been done, it was quite easy to remove all the symptoms in one hypnosis, but it was evident from the circumstances of the case that it was purely a matter of chance that more serious injury had not been done.

A public objection has been raised against the use of hypnotism on the ground that a person may be hypnotised against his or her will. This is an entire fallacy. *The consent of the subject is always necessary.* To prove this, I have requested some of my deepest subjects to refuse their consent, with the result that my efforts to hypnotise them have been entirely in vain.

Lastly, it is supposed by some that from the time a person is hypnotised he is under the influence of the operator, and that for his whole life he will be at his bidding. This idea is completely untrue. We find others believing that the hypnotist can even influence his patients at a distance, and by the simple concentration of will control their thoughts and actions wherever they may be.[1]

Such ideas as these are really too absurd to deny; there is some excuse, however, for persons holding this view; since many of the charlatans who combined with their stock-in-trade a certain amount of mesmerism, electro-biology, etc., used to assert that all these things were possible.

Thus, the common notions concerning hypnotism have no basis of fact. They not only are incredible by any sane mind, but also tend to hinder a consideration of the real dangers of hypnotism.

These dangers I proceed to enumerate. And firstly, on the relation of hypnotism to crime; this has to be considered because, as we have seen in

---

[1] I have already referred, tentatively, to the general question of telepathy. This must not be confused with the fiction just mentioned.

the earlier portion of this book, some persons are so deeply influenced that they become entirely obedient to the hypnotist. They are absolutely insensible to pain, and on waking can remember nothing of anything which may have happened in hypnosis.

It is clear that such a state presents possibilities of crime, but it is to be remembered that according to all the observations of Liébault, Bernheim, etc., only about fifteen per cent. of subjects are influenced to this deep degree, which is termed Somnambulism. Nevertheless, however small the number, the fact that it is possible for a criminal action to be proposed or a criminal suggestion made with success, justifies a consideration of the matter.

This question of the criminal use of hypnotism recently came before the public in the "Gouffé murder trial." Gabrille Bompard, as is well known, set up the defence that her part in the tragedy was due to post-hypnotic suggestions given to her by her paramour, Michel Eyraud. A large amount of evidence was called on both sides, but the jury refused to accept the defence put forward, and returned a verdict of guilty.

Then there is the liability to assault, a possibility which, in the case of female subjects, is obviously of the greatest possible importance. Several cases, where a criminal assault has been committed, have been reported in various countries. On this point the remedy is easy, and should be put in force by the operator for the sake of his own responsibility, and by the subject for her safety and confidence. Dr Kingsbury sums this up well by saying, "No person should permit himself or herself to be hypnotised save by a medical man (or properly authorised scientist) who has a character to maintain, and in whose integrity and ability confidence can be reposed. And further, no woman should allow herself to be hypnotised except in the presence of one or more witnesses of whom she approves."[1]

The possibilities of criminal suggestion have been elaborately discussed by many writers, prominent amongst whom are Gilles de la Tourette, Liégois, and Forel.

It is admitted by all that even amongst somnambulists the proportion who would commit a crime in response to suggestion is almost *infinitesimal*. For not only will the subject refuse to commit a crime, but it has been often noticed that any suggestion, which is repulsive to the feelings of the patient, will, in all probability, be disobeyed.

Liégois narrates amongst many others the following case :—

"I dissolved a white powder in water, and solemnly declared to Madame C— (a patient aged thirty-five) that it was arsenic. I then said to her

[1] *The Practice of Hypnotic Suggestion*, p. 119.

'Here is Monsieur D—, he is thirsty, he will ask you in a moment for something to drink: you will offer him this glass of water.' 'Yes, sir.' Monsieur D—, however, asked a question I had not foreseen: he asked what was in the glass. And with a candour that banished all idea of simulation, Madam C— replied: 'It is arsenic!' I was therefore obliged to correct my suggestion, and I said, 'If you are asked what the glass contains, you will say sugar and water.'

"Cross-questioned by the commissary of police, Madame C— remembers absolutely nothing. She asserts that she has seen nothing, done nothing, and not given anything to drink to any one: she does not know what they mean."

Gilles de la Tourette records another experiment of criminal suggestion:—

"We first put H. E—, who has had some words with our friend B—, a medical student in the hospital, into a state of somnambulism, we then say to him: 'You know Monsieur B—?' 'Yes, sir.' 'He is a very nice man!' 'Oh no, sir, he does not attend to me properly!' 'Really! well then we must put him out of the way, and then we shall certainly have another student who will take better care of you.' 'I ask for nothing better.' 'You must do what is necessary: here is a pistol (and we place a ruler in his hand); when you awake, you will fire at him, he will be coming here, wait for him!'

"We blow on H. E—'s eyes, who, after awaking, continues conversing with us, all the while playing with the revolver (or rather the ruler that represents a revolver in his eyes); which he absolutely refuses to part with. The suggestion not yet having been fulfilled, the subject would sooner kill any one who tried to dispossess him of his weapon, rather than give it up.

"At a certain moment our friend B—, who has been warned of the way he will be greeted, enters the ward. H. E— allows him to approach, and then coolly discharges his pistol point blank at him. B— falls down, exclaiming: 'I am killed!' 'What,' we say to H. E—, 'you have killed Monsieur B—! but what can have induced you to commit such a crime?' 'Monsieur B—, did not properly attend to me; I have revenged myself!' 'That is not a sufficient reason.' 'You may think so, but I had also many others; besides, he was doomed to die by my hand!'"

Dr Luys of the Charity Hospital, Paris, in one of his "Clinical Lectures on Hypnotism," says—

"You can not only oblige this defenceless being, who is incapable of opposing the slightest resistance, to give from hand to hand anything you may choose, but you can also make him sign a promise, draw up a bill of exchange, or any other kind of agreement. You may make him write an holographic will (which according to French law would be valid), which he will hand over to you, and of which he will *never know the existence*. He is ready to fulfil the minutest legal formalities, and will do so with a calm, serene, and natural manner calculated to deceive the most expert law officers. The somnambulists will not hesitate either, you may be sure, to make a denunciation, or to bear false witness; they are, I repeat, the passive instruments of your will. For instance, take E—: she will at my bidding write out and sign a donation of forty pounds in my favour. In a criminal point of view, the subject under certain suggestions will make false denunciations, accuse this or that person, and maintain with the greatest assurance that he has assisted at an imaginary crime. I will recall to your mind those scenes of fictitious assassination, which I have exhibited before you.

"I was careful to place in the subject's hand a piece of paper instead of a dagger or a revolver; but it is evident, that if they had held veritable murderous instruments, the scene might have had a tragic ending."

It must be remembered that all these experiments which have been made were surrounded with circumstances which would convince the subject of a want of reality.

There is no doubt that subjects may be induced to commit all sorts of imaginary crimes in one's study (Moll). These "laboratory experiments" prove nothing, because some trace of consciousness always remains to tell the subject that the crime, though he may feel bound to commit it, is not criminal. This may seem paradoxical; but I think the observation is confirmed by almost every operator that there is present in at any rate 99 per cent. of hypnotised persons a *certain latent moral consciousness* which will prevent the success of any suggestion repugnant to their tastes, religion, or morals.

Still, from the experiments of Liégois, and others, it seems as if there were a very small class who could be induced to commit a real crime.

Many other possibilities of suggestion may occur, such, for instance, as the suggestion that the subject on waking should write a cheque or make a will in the operator's favour.

In all this it will be seen that—

1. Only the smallest percentage of subjects are at all likely to be obedient to the suggestion.
2. The manner of carrying out the act is likely to betray the fact that they are acting under post-hypnotic suggestion.
3. The operator himself runs into great danger; for, on the subject being hypnotised by some one else, the whole facts of the case might be ascertained.

Nevertheless, it is important that every one

should recognise that the dangers of hypnotism in the hands of the ignorant, the unscrupulous, or the malicious, are real; and though it would be idle to attack hypnotism itself because, like everything else, it is open to abuse, yet the public have a right to demand that they should have some guarantee that the qualifications of the hypnotist and his good faith are unquestionable.

Both for the sake of the science, and for the sake of the public weal, it is imperative that proper restrictions should be placed on the use of hypnotism. If a man be not allowed to practise as a physician or a surgeon without having first given satisfactory evidence of his qualifications, still more in the case of hypnotism, where his power for good and his power for evil is so great, should the law intervene, that the good be encouraged and the evil prevented.

I conclude this chapter by giving the rules which Prof. Bernheim, writing as a physician on the therapeutic side of hypnotism, lays down :—[1]

1. "Never hypnotise any subject without his formal consent, or the consent of those in authority over him.

2. "Never induce sleep except in the presence of a third person in authority, who can guarantee the good faith of the hypnotist and the subject. Thus any trouble may be avoided in the event of an accusation, or any suspicion of an attempt which is not for the relief of the subject.

[1] Op. cit., p. 416.

3. "Never give to the hypnotised subject, without his consent, any other suggestions than those necessary for his case. The physician has no rights but those conferred upon him by the patient. He should limit himself to the therapeutic suggestion; any other experiment is forbidden him, without the formal consent of the patient, even if it be in the interest of science. The physician should not profit by his authority over the patient in order to provoke this consent, if he think that the experiment which he wishes to perform may have the slightest harmful effect."

The presence of responsible witnesses whenever hypnosis is induced would practically prevent the possibility of any criminal or illicit use of hypnotism; and if this little book can, in any way, impress on the public mind the urgent necessity for some such legal restrictions and safeguards, it will not have been written altogether in vain.

CHAPTER VII.

THE VALUES OF HYPNOTISM.

The word "suggestion"—Nature of mind affected—Nervous diseases—Cases of Dr Bernheim—Dumontpallier—Buckhardt—Voisin—Van Eeden—Binot—Velander—Osgood—Van Renterghem and Van Eeden—Delboeuf—Lloyd Tuckey—Kingsbury—Felkin—Nature of cures effected.

WHILST the study of hypnotism has been and will continue to be of the greatest value in all psychological matters, it has a greater claim on the attention of the crowd since it has shown itself to be of such enormous importance in medicine. With this medical aspect I am quite unqualified to deal on my own account, and I am the more unwilling to dabble in a science, not my own, since some valuable works on this part of the subject have been published.

We have already referred to the action of the mind on the body, under its normal and abnormal conditions, and it has been seen that this mental influence is capable of producing the greatest physical changes. It is the object of the medical hypnotist to induce a state in which the mind is most receptive of suggestion and in which that suggestion will be acted on with the greatest promptitude and certainty. The *bête noire* of all writers, on this subject of mental influence, is the popular confusion which exists between imaginary disease and diseases of the imagination.

There is no such thing as an imaginary disease. If a man persist in thinking from Monday morning to Saturday night that he is seriously ill, the very fact that he has this impression is clear proof that either his mind or his body is diseased or out of health. It is only the idle or the stupid physician who would give no heed to a patient because it is the "imagination" or "will" which is at fault.

"Suggestion" is just now the fashionable term used by a number of ordinary medical men, who happen to have read, or perhaps only heard of some primer of hypnotism; and, apparently, there are many who think that this word is quite sufficient to account for any change. The word, however, at any rate in English, is really a very weak one, and in no sense conveys the meaning in which it is used by hypnotists. By "suggestion," as it is used in ordinary life, we mean a piece of advice or an hint offered; by "suggestion" in hypnotism we mean an impression made on the mind which will result in an immediate adaptation of the brain and all it controls to that impression. There is, moreover, a great distinction between the use of "suggestion" in the waking and in the hypnotic state. Used in the waking, it is generally only impressionable, emotional, and weak-minded persons who can be affected directly by it; whilst, as Dr Moll says, no patient, be he ever so intelligent, can resist the influence of hypnotic suggestion, if only the hypnosis be deep enough, and, as a matter of fact, the more intelligent the patient, the more he is susceptible.

If an hypnotist want to practise his skill by experiments in difficult cases, he will choose the dull, the stupid, and the ignorant as his subjects.

A common misunderstanding, also, with regard to the curative powers of hypnotism, exists in the idea that only "nervous ailments" are to be benefitted. On the other hand, the medical hypnotists for some long time have been reporting cases of cure in organic diseases, which thoroughly overthrow the supposition that nervous disorders are the only ones affected by hypnotism.

Judging from these reports, it may be fairly said that there is no ailment which cannot be to some extent alleviated by means of hypnotic suggestion; whilst many of the functional disturbances, which have persistently baffled all attempts of the medical profession, have succumbed to hypnotism. As this is in no sense a medical work, I cannot enlarge on the whole of the value and use of hypnosis; but it has such an important bearing on the values of hypnotism that it will hardly be out of place to give the reader some idea of the nature of the cures effected. I therefore append some typical observations, reported by authorities of the highest reputation in the medical profession, whose honesty and good faith are beyond all question. Dr Bernheim, in his now famous treatise "Suggestive Therapeutics," devotes a large part of his work to a minute description of the various cases which have come before him; in this way an hundred typical observations are recorded. The particulars are of interest only to the medical world, and I therefore will simply give a list of the observations as recorded at the end of his book.

A.—*Organic diseases of the nervous system:* 10.

1. Cerebral hemorrhage, hemiplegia, hemianæsthesia with tremor and contracture. *Cure.*
2. Cerebro-spinal disease; apoplectiform attacks, paralyses, ulnar neuritis. *Cure.*
3. Partial left hemiplegia. *Cure.*
4. Traumatic epilepsy, with traumatic rheumatism. *Cure.*
5. Sensory organic hemianæsthesia. *Cure.*
6. Diffuse rheumatic myelitis. *Improvement.*
7. Cerebro-spinal insular sclerosis. *Marked Improvement for six months.*
8. Nervous troubles (organic cause?) in the brachial plexus. Temporary suppression of the symptoms. *No cure.*

THE VALUES OF HYPNOTISM. 239

9. Paresis, of traumatic origin, of the muscles of the hand. *Cure.*
10. Paresis of the extensors of the hand and saturnine anæthesia. *Cure.*

B.—*Hysterical diseases:* 17.

11. Hystero-epilepsy in a man, sensitivo-sensorial hemianæsthesia. *Cure.*
12. Hysteria, sensitivo-sensorial anæsthesia. Transient suppression of the symptoms. *No Cure.*
13. Hemiplegia, with left sensitivo-sensorial hemianæsthesia. *Cure.*
14. Hysterical sensitivo-sensorial hemianæsthesia. *Cure.*
15. Hysteriform paroxsyms with hysterical somnambulism. *Cure.*
16. Anæsthesia; hysterical spinal pain. *Cure.*
17. Paralysis, with hysterical anæsthesia. *Cure.*
18. Convulsive hysteria, with hemianæsthesia. *Cure.*
19. Hysteria; paroxsyms of convulsive weeping. *Cure.*
20. Convulsive hysteria. *Cure.*
21. Convulsive hysteria, with hemianæsthesia. *Cure.*
22. Convulsive hysteria. *Cure.*
23. Convulsive hysteria, with hemianæsthesia. *Cure.*
24. Convulsive hysteria, with hemianæsthesia. *Cure.*
25. Hysteria, with hemianæsthesia. *Cure.*

26. Hysteria in the male; weeping and convulsive paroxsyms. *Cure* (at least temporary).
27. Hysterical aphonia. *Cure.*

C.—*Neuropathic affections:* 18.

28. Nervous aphonia. *Cure.*
29. Moral inertia, with subjective sensations in the head. *Cure.*
30. Nervous aphonia. *Cure.*
31. Post-epileptic tremor, cephalagia and insomnia. *Cure.*
32. Nervous gastric troubles; anæsthesia. *Improvement.*
33. Neuropathic pains. *Cure.*
34. Epigastric pains. *Cure.*
35. Neuropathic lumbar pains; insomnia. *Cure.*
36. Paresis, with sense of weight in the right leg. *Cure.*
37. Pains in the right leg. *Cure.*
38. Girdle-pain and pain in right groin, with difficulty in walking, for twenty months. *Cure.*
39. Insomnia, loss of appetite, mental depression, tremor. *Cure.*
40. Gloomy ideas, insomnia, loss of appetite. *Cure.*
41. Insomnia through habit. *Partial Cure.*
42. Cephalalgia; intellectual obnubilation. *Cure.*
43. Vertigo, moral depression connected with cardiac disease. *Cure.*

44. Laziness, disobedience, and loss of appetite in a child. *Cure.*
45. Pseudo-paraplegia with tremor. *Cure.*

D.—*Various neuroses:* 15.

46. Choreic movements consecutive to chorea. *Cure.*
47. Id. id. id.
48. Choreic movements from moral emotion. *Cure.*
49. Post-choreic tremor in the hand. *Cure.*
50. Post-choreic trouble in writing. *Cure.*
51. Choreic movements in the hands. *Cure.*
52. Hemi-chorea; rapid improvement. *Gradual cure.*
53. General chorea. *Gradual cure.*
54. Id. id.
55. Obstinate writer's cramp. Rapid improvement. *Gradual cure.*
56. Attacks of tetany, nocturnal somnambulism. *Cure.*
57. Nocturnal somnambulism. *Temporary cure.*
58. Nocturnal enuresis. *Cure.*
59. Id. id. id.
60. Nocturnal enuresis; aphonia consecutive to pneumonia. *Cure.*

E.—*Dynamic pareses and paralyses:* 3.

61. Sense of weight, with paresis of the left arm. *Cure.*

62. Dynamic psychical paraplegia. *Cure.*
63. Pains and paresis of the lower limbs. *Cure.*

F.—Gastro-intestinal affections : 4.

64. Alcoholic gastritis, with insomnia and weakness of the legs. *Improvement.*
65. Chronic gastritis; diatation of the stomach and vomiting. *Improvement.*
66. Gastric troubles; burning sensation over sternum; insomnia. *Cure.*
67. Gastro-intestinal catarrh; metritis; neuropathy. *Improvement.*

G.—Various painful affections : 12.

68. Epigastric pain. *Cure.*
69. Umbilical and epigastric pain. *Cure.*
70. Interscapular pain. *Cure.*
71. Thoracic pain; insomnia (Tubercular diathesis). *Cure.*
72. Hypogastric and supra-inguinal pains on the left side connected with an old pelvic-peritonitis. *Cure.*
73. Intercostal pain. *Cure.*
74. Thoracic pain. *Gradual cure.*
75. Painful contusion of the deltoid. *Cure.*
76. Muscular pain in the flank. *Cure.*
77. Painful spot in the side. *Cure.*
78. Pains in the epitrochlear muscles. *Cure.*

79. Pain in the shoulder and upper right limb from effort. *Cure.*

H.—*Rheumatic affections:* 19.

80. Rheumatic paralysis of the right fore-arm. *Cure.*
81. Rheumatic scapulo-humeral arthritis. *Improvement without cure.*
82. Muscular rheumatism with cramp. *Cure.*
83. Ilio-lumbar rheumatic neuralgia. *Cure.*
84. Arthralgia consecutive to an arthritis. *Cure.*
85. Pleurodynia and lumbar pain helped by suggestion. *Cure.*
86. Apyretic articular rheumatism. *Gradual cure.*
87. Chronic articular rheumatism (wrists and insteps). *Cure.*
88. Muscular articular and nervous rheumatism. *Gradual cure.*
89. Acromio-clavicular and xiphoid rheumatic pains. *Cure.*
90. Muscular lumbo-crural rheumatism, with sacro-sciatic neuralgia. *Rapid improvement; almost total cure.*
91. Apyretic articular rheumatism. *Gradual cure.*
92. Acromio-clavicular rheumatic pains. *Cure.*
93. Muscular rheumatism in the arm and right leg. *Cure.*
94. Gonorrheal rheumatism. *Gradual cure.*

95. Acromio-clavicular and xiphoid articular rheumatism. *Cure.*
96. Rheumatic articular pains. *Cure.*
97. Dorsal and metacarpo-phalangeal rheumatic pains. *Cure.*
98. Rheumatic, dorso-lumbar, and sciatic pains. *Cure.*

I.—*Neuralgias:* 5.

99. Rebellious sciatica. *Cure.*
100. Recent sciatica helped by one suggestion. *Cure.*
101. Rebellious sciatica. *Cure.*
102. Rebellious sciatica. *Gradual cure.*
103. Neuralgia of the trigeminus with facial *tic douloureux. Almost complete cure.*[1]

Dr Lloyd Tuckey has compiled a list of some typical cases from which I take some examples:—

1. Hysterical contracture of the leg.[2] *Cured.*
2. Aggravated hypochondriasis.[3] *Cured.*
3. Acute puerperal mania.[4] *Cured.*
4. Hysteria, tendency to tetaniform spasms, insomnia, morphia and chloral habit.[5] *Cured.*

---

[1] Bernheim, op. cit., p. 404 *et seq.*
[2] Dumontpallier (Physician to the Hotel Dieu, Paris). Revue de l' Hypnotisme. April 1890.
[3] Buckhardt (superintendent of the asylum at Préfargier). Revue de l' Hypnotisme. Aug. 1888.
[4] Buckhardt. *Ibid.*
[5] Buckhardt, *loc. cit.*

5. Moral depravity in a boy.[1] *Cured.*
6. Neuralgia of the neck and left shoulder; paralysis of the left arm and leg, of syphilitic origin.[2] *Cured.*
7. Cephelalgia, gastrodynia, dyspepsia.[3] *Cured.*
8. Chronic alcoholism[4] (over sixteen years' duration, patient had suffered from several attacks of *delirium tremens*). *Cured.*
9. Neurasthenia, with deficiency of saliva and constipation for thirty-five years.[5] *Cured.*
10. Functional dumbness, with melancholy.[6] *Cured.*
11. Functional paraplegia and hemi-anæsthesia.[7] *Greatly benefited.*
12. Epilepsy. *Cured.*
    Do. *Cured.*
    Do. *Cured.*
    Do.[8] *Cured.*
13. Intermittent fever.[9] *Cured.*
14. Syphilitic retinitis with optic neuritis.[10] *Greatly improved.*

---

[1] Voisin. Revue de l' Hypnotisme. Nov. 1888.
[2] Contributed by Van Eeden (Amsterdam).
[3] Van Eeden.
[4] Van Eeden.
[5] Burot, Rochefort. Revue de l' Hypnotisme. Dec. 1888.
[6] Velander (Yonkoping, Sweden).
[7] Osgood. *Boston Medical and Surgical Journal,* June 1890.
[8] All four cases contributed by Bérillon (*Revue de l' Hypnotisme,* Oct. 1890).
[9] Van Renterghem and Van Eeden.
[10] Delbœuf (Liège).

Dr Tuckey's own work has been so important that my quotations would be very incomplete did they not include his observations. I am much indebted to him for the trouble and time spent in showing me his own methods. A selection from his cases follows; the reader who wishes for more will find these and others fully discussed in Dr Tuckey's book, "Psycho-Therapeutics."[1]

1. Torticollis, etc. *Cured.*
2. Chronic diarrhœa. *Cured.*
3. Paroxysmal sneezing. *Cured.*
4. Chronic constipation. *Cured.*
5. Supra-orbital neuralgia. *Cured.*
6. Spinal irritation. *Cured.*
7. Functional heart-trouble. *Cured.*
8. Symptoms dependent on mitral disease. *Cured.*
9. Nocturnal eneuresis. *Cured.*
10. Chronic rheumatism. *Cured.*
11. Nervous dyspepsia. *Cured.*
12. Amenorrhœa. *Cured.*
13. Functional dysmenorrhœa. *Cured.*
14. Dipsomania. *Cured.*
15. Tobacco habit. *Cured.*
16. Neurasthenia. *Cured.*
17. Chronic alcoholism. *Cured.*
18. Nervous prostration. *Cured.*
19. Extreme anæmia. *Cured.*

[1] See also "The Value of Hypnotism in Chronic Alcoholism." Tuckey. London, 1892.

I also append a few cases from those recorded by Dr Kingsbury.[1]

1. Obstinate neuralgia in the tongue, and morphonomaniac tendency. *Cured.*
2. Insomnia, with great mental depression. *Cured.*
3. Melancholia and hypochondriasis. *Cured.*
4. Muscular rheumatism, with ulcerations of the throat. *Cured.*
5. Menorrhagia. *Cured.*
6. Inebriety. *Cured.*
7. Stammering. *Cured.*
8. Contraction of the Palmar Fascia. *Cured.*
9. Rheumatism in the hip. *Cured.*
10. Chronic anæmic headache, with insomnia. *Cured.*
11. Chronic constipation. *Cured.*
12. Pains in the chest, mental depression, palpitation. *Cured.*
13. Melancholia, insomnia, dyspepsia. *Cured.*
14. Asthma (of several years' duration). *Cured.*
15. "Brain-fog." *Cured.*
16. Neurasthenia. *Cured.*
17. Sub-acute rheumatism. *Cured.*
18. Hepatic pain. *Cured.*
19. Neurasthenia. *Cured.*
20. "Pulsating spine." *Cured.*
21. Dysmenorrhea. *Cured.*
22. Painful variocele. *Cured.*

[1] "Practice of Hypnotic Suggestion." Bristol, 1891.

23. Cocaine and morphia mania. *Cured for a time. Finally the patient relapsed.*
24. Moral perversion in a child.[1] *Cured.*
25. Rheumatic contraction of fingers. *Cured.*
26. Inebriety (ten years' duration). *Cured.*

An host of cases might be quoted, but it is unnecessary, in a non-medical work, to go through the enormous list of them. I have but one more list to

---

[1] So many cases of this kind have been chronicled by various authorities, that were it not for the reputation of the writers, it would be difficult to believe some of the statements. I quote Dr Kingsbury's description of the case :—

S. T. aged eight, had for a couple of years given her parents the greatest anxiety, owing to the most unaccountable paroxysms of malicious conduct, during which she was more like a youthful maniac than a naughty girl. She would in the most deliberate and cool manner plan how to inflict bodily pain on others. For example, she would go up to her nurse and caress her, and while the servant was reciprocating the apparent affection, would suddenly strike her in the abdomen with all the strength she could muster. At other times she would lie awake for hours, all the while feigning sleep, and when her mother was asleep, she would leave her own bed, and climb on to that of her mother, and kick her on the breast as hard as she could. As a result of one of these midnight attacks, the mother had a swelling in one breast, which she feared would develop into cancer. This child was particularly muscular, and seemed herself to be almost insensible to pain ; she would laugh if she were flogged, and say she liked it. Every means had been exhausted in the attempt to correct this girl's habits, thrashing, seclusion, cold shower baths, low diet, etc., but all to no purpose. She became more violent and callous, and absolutely disobedient.

Her parents thought her "possessed of a devil," and dreaded her growing up, fearing that she would end in an asylum, or on the gallows.

After one hypnotic sitting, the child's character was completely revolutionised ; she became obedient, gentle, loving, and thoughtful for others.

THE VALUES OF HYPNOTISM.

refer to, and that is a table which has been adapted from Dr Felkin's book on the medical uses of hypnotism, and this classification is a potent illustration of its therapeutic value.

	No. of Cases.	Cured.	Improved.	Failed.
Organic Diseases of the Nervous System,	10 B. 24 R. 1 T.	7 B. 1 R. 1 T.	2 B. 13 R. ...	1 B. 10 R. ...
Hysterical Diseases,	17 B. 36 R.	16 B. 9 R.	... 24 R.	1 B. 3 R.
Neuropathic Affections,	18 B. 145 R. 1 W. 1 T.	17 B. 47 R. 1 W. 1 T.	1 B. 76 R.	... 22 R. ... ...
Various Neuroses,	15 B. 4 T.	14 B. 4 T.	1 B. ...	... ...
Dynamic Pareses and Paralyses,	3 B. 1 T.	3 B. 1 T.	... ...	... ...
Gastro-intestinal Affections,	4 B. 1 T.	1 B. 1 T.	3 B. ...	... ...
Various Painful Affections,	12 B. 15 R. 2 T.	12 B. 2 R. 2 T.	... 6 R. ...	... 7 R. ...
Rheumatic Affections,	19 B. 23 R.	17 B. 7 R.	2 B. 14 R.	... 2 R.
Neuralgias,	5 B. 57 R.	4 B. 17 R.	1 B. 30 R.	... 10 R.
Amenorrhœa,	13 V.	13 V.	...	...
Dysmenorrhœa,	6 V. 1 T.	6 V. 1 T.	... ...	... ...
Menorrhagia,	8 V. 1 F.	8 V. 1 F.	... ...	... ...
Mental Diseases,	53 R.	10 R.	27 R.	16 R.
Totals,	496	224	200	72

B., Bernheim; R., Van Renterghem and Van Eeden; T., Tuckey; W., Wagner; V., Various authors.[1]

In quoting the observations of the physicians, as I have done, I may incur the peculiarly odious

[1] Op. cit., p. 57.

suspicion of quackery. On my behalf I must plead that the medical works are generally confined to the medical world, and, in matters so important to all, it seems not altogether unfitting that others should be able to form some idea of the value and the scope of hypnotism in its therapeutic application. The lists which I have given do not exaggerate the benefits of this application, since in the successful cases there is no mention of the time taken in the cure. Such passages as the following are of constant occurrence in the reports of the physicians:—

"He ridiculed the idea of hypnotism helping him, but was soon affected, though only to a slight degree. . . . He was only hypnotised twice, but at the end of three weeks reported that he was quite cured, sleeping every night like a child, and enjoying his days. He said he would gladly have given ten years off his life for the relief he had obtained." Or,

"He was only hypnotised once; but at the end of nine weeks, wrote to say that he had, ever since his hypnosis, felt 'quite another man, able to do any amount of work and enjoy life.'"

A most curious and important fact is that a very large proportion of the cures chronicled are cures of diseases regarded as practically incurable or "chronic." In the table taken from Dr Felkin, we have a list of 496 cases, of which 224 were absolutely cured and 200 improved; or 424 cases of success and benefit to 72 failures.

It is not wonderful that the village doctor and the easy-going parish practitioner know nothing of these things, and view with suspicion and ignorant intolerance the attempt of the foremost medical men to introduce hypnotism into their science; nor indeed would it be desirable for any concerned that these comfortable ornaments of their several parishes should be at all imbued with the hypnotic ideas. A little knowledge is a dangerous thing.

CHAPTER VIII.

THE "TRANSFER" EXPERIMENTS.

A LARGE amount of public attention has been directed to some "hypnotic" experiments connected with La Charité Hospital, Paris, of which Dr Luys is the physician. Dr Luys himself first put these theories before English readers in two articles in the *Fortnightly Review* for June and August 1890, entitled, "The Recent Discoveries in Hypnotism." By this curious method the patient himself is not sent to sleep, but another is hypnotised, and then by means of a magnet the disease is "transferred" from the patient who is awake to the hypnotised subject, who before she is awakened is freed by suggestion from the effects. This idea is by no means a "discovery," for, many years ago, something very similar was a favourite doctrine of the mesmerists, who found, according to their accounts, that, when the patients were mesmerised, their pains were experienced for a time by the mesmerist.

The influence of the magnet in the curing of disease was firmly believed in by many of the ancients. Hippocrates strongly advocated its use, and there are tomes of mediæval lore concerning the magnetic virtues (*Vide* Kircher, Maxwell, and others). In 1845, Reichenbach published an elaborate account of the action of magnets on the human organism; so that, altogether, Dr Luys' "discoveries" were somewhat ancient.

However, despite the fact that the main theory of Dr Luys is almost as old as the hills, it may be well to examine his experiments.

Luys tells us that, " This new method of therapeutics consists in the transference of the nervous state of a diseased subject, to a subject hypnotised, by means of a magnetic rod." (*A* is the patient wide awake.) "*A* lays his hands on those of the sleeping subject, and an assistant, holding a big magnetised rod with three branches, moves it for a minute or two in front of the arms of the two persons placed before him. He follows the lines of the limbs, forming thus a circuit of continuous magnetisation, and, at the same time, he takes good care only to work with the north pole (this is of vital importance) when he stops at the painful places pointed out by the patient."

Not only will the hypnotised subject take the disease of the patient, but also the personality, so that when a female subject is sitting for a male patient, she will assume a masculine voice and carriage, and will complain of the beard being pulled if her face be touched. A few facts concerning these strange methods may serve to show the probable explanation.

1. The subjects are all hysterical.
2. The same set of subjects are in daily attendance at the laboratory.
3. They are paid by the patients whose ailments they are supposed to take, and they attend solely for the sake of these gratuities.
4. They are always about the laboratory, so that they can see exactly what is expected of them by seeing the other transfer operations.
5. All these subjects regularly read the history of the cases as published in the clinical reports of the hospital.
6. The ailment is *seen* to be adopted by the subject if it be an apparent one, such as paralysis; it is *assumed* to be transferred if it be not a visible complaint, such as heart-disease.
7. The patient, in many cases, does not appear to be any better when his transfer is effected. Thus a patient suffering from "paralysis agitans" may have his affection "transferred" to the subject, who will adopt the most violent palsy; but all this time the patient is suffering still.[1]

It is plain from these facts that the suffering of the subject is due to the suggestion made that he should

---

[1] *Vide* Kingsbury, op. cit., p. 147.

suffer, whilst in the cases where the patient is really benefited the cause clearly lies in the effect which the sight of the subject undergoing his or her suffering would necessarily have on a person of impressionable temperament and vivid imagination. Another of Luys' theories is that the magnet can produce emotional effects. The argument is, that as the north pole of a magnet attracts the needle, while the south repels it, so in human beings similar emotions are excited.

"If you present the *north* pole of a magnetic rod to a subject in a state of lethargy, you arouse in him movements of *joy* and expansion of feeling; and if you connect him with the *south* pole, movements of *repulsion* appear."

There might be some test in these experiments, since the subject, we might think, would be ignorant as to which was the north pole and which the south, and thus suggestion would be eliminated. Unfortunately, however, a large "N," almost an inch high, written in blue ink, was placed on the north pole.

The subjects are also supposed to see flames issuing from the magnet, of a beautiful *yellow* light from the *north* pole, and a *blue* light from the *south* pole.

Reichenbach's subjects found that the colours of the "odylic light" at the *north* pole were *blue*, and *yellow* at the *south*.

Many other experiments of Luys might be

described, such for instance as the influence of drugs in sealed tubes, where by contact alone the appropriate reactions are brought about, brandy producing intoxication, etc., etc.

Transference of Sensation. One class of experiments in La Charité have provided a great deal of "copy," of a cheap kind, for several newspapers. This consists in taking a glass of water or a doll, and then transferring the sensation of the subject to the water or the doll. In consequence of this "transference," if the water be touched or the doll pinched, the subject experiences the most acute agony, and groans until the water or the doll, as the case may be, is left alone. Here again suggestion is the explanation. Recently I gave a demonstration of the fallacies of these experiments and the following was the report:—

"The subject was now introduced, and being thrown into the hypnotic state, the experiment was tried with complete success. Whenever the water was touched, *and the subject was aware of the fact*, he shuddered and writhed until the features became distorted as if with excessive pain. When, however, the water was touched and the patient was kept in ignorance of the fact, there was no effect whatever upon him."

No reference would have been made to these experiments at Paris, since it seems the more scientific and their better deserved treatment to ignore them; but I have been so constantly requested to explain these "newspaper" phenomena, that it seems better to briefly notice them—for, I trust, the last time.

CHAPTER IX.

HYPNOSIS IN ANIMALS.

THE hypnotisation of animals is possible to a very limited extent, and indeed it is not altogether accurate to term the condition, induced, hypnosis; there is, of course, no receptivity to suggestion, and all we can obtain is a certain rigidity, so that the animal, bird, or reptile, will remain in any position in which it may be placed. Apparently the first one to notice this phenomenon was Daniel Schwenter, who in 1636 catalepsed a number of cocks and hens. Fr. Kircher (1646) was the first to make any scientific experiments on the subject. He took fowls, and having tied their legs together, placed them on the ground, and he then drew a chalk line from their beaks, with the result that the birds remained perfectly motionless. A hen can be made to sit or to transfer her nest by means of a well-known expedient. The head is placed under the wings, and the bird is then rocked gently to and fro, with the result that it apparently goes to sleep; on waking, the hen will remain contentedly in the nest on which she has been placed.

The Fakirs and the Aïssouans are reported to be able to fascinate the most venomous snakes, to charm them with music, and induce the snake to imitate, as far as possible, their movements.

All these tales require a great deal of sober corroboration before they can be regarded as of any value. It is well known that in the case of the snake-charmers, the fangs of the snakes have been extracted.

The catalepsy induced in animals by nerve stimulation has been compared to the fascination which it is said many animals can exercise over others. Of this fascination there can hardly be any doubt. I have frequently seen frogs and little birds fascinated by a snake; but it is by no means the rule. Out of an hundred frogs which were put into my snake case, only six were in any sense fascinated; the others jumped about madly till they were caught by the snakes.

It seems rash to compare this fascination, which may be the natural consequence of extreme fright, with the catalepsy induced by means of pressure on the nerves.

Many such illustrations are given as analogous instances. It is not easy to catch a pigeon by going straight up to the bird, but it can be quickly taken by walking round and round it. The pigeon turns upon itself, so as not to lose sight of the person who is trying to catch it, and can soon be seized. This has been quoted as an hypnosis. The obvious explanation seems to be that the bird was rendered giddy and dazed.

Many animals may be rendered obedient and docile by means of the fixed look and movements which will tend to concentrate their attention. I am confident of being able to prevent the most vicious dog from attacking me so long as I can keep my eyes on him. On one occasion I succeeded in compelling a "jibbing" horse to "back," by simply fixing my eyes on his, and then walking towards him; on my taking my eyes from him, he, glad to be released, immediately started off in the proper direction, and the driver, on that journey, had no more difficulty with him.

A phenomenon which seems allied to the catalepsy induced by nerve stimulation is seen in the *simulated death* of many animals.

Insects of many kinds, spiders, crayfish, etc., fall into a state of complete insensibility the moment they are alarmed, but they recover directly the exciting cause of the alarm is removed (Romanes).

The cataleptic state is induced in animals either by the monotonous excitation of particular nerves, or by constant pressure. The operation, in some cases, is easy, in others, difficult; whilst in the larger animals it seems generally impossible, owing to the great resistance made at the outset.

FIG. 16.—*Frog Catalepsed* (p. 261).

FIG. 17.—*Frog Catalepsed* (p. 261).

Fig. 18.—*Snake Catalepsed* (p. 261).

Fig. 19.—*Toad Catalepsed* (p. 261).

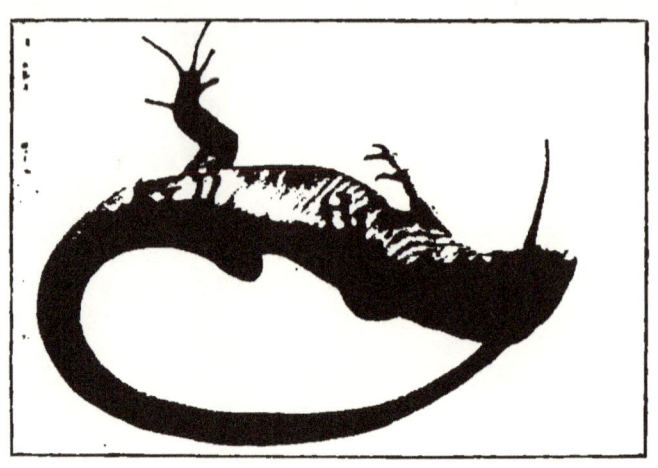

FIG. 20.—*Lizard Catalepsed* (p. 261).

By means of simple nerve inhibition, I have catalepsed cats (rarely), dogs (less rarely, but not often), pigeons, canaries, fowls, starlings, crayfish, frogs (Figs. 16 and 17), snakes (Fig. 18), toads (Fig. 19), lizards (Fig. 20), slow-worms, etc., etc.

It appears likely that, with instruments for applying the proper stimulation and pressure, catalepsy could be induced in the larger animals, such as the horse and the bullock.

There seems, however, little of scientific value in the "hypnosis" of animals, except as a possible explanation of the phenomena due in the man to concentrated attention. This animal catalepsy is induced from outside when produced by means of nerve stimulation; the *simulated death*, however, of which many insects are capable, is evidently an act of the brain in its highest centres. Here, then, we have the phenomenon of unconsciousness to the external produced by simple mental action.

On the other hand, when we are dealing with the catalepsy induced by nerve excitation, we seem to find some analogy to the hypnoses induced by means of a sudden flash of light or the unexpected sounding of a loud gong.

APPENDIX.

Note 1.

The works of Father Athanasius Kircher cover an enormous ground. There has been founded in Rome a Museum named after him. The following is the title-page of his work, quoted on page 6 :—

"Athanasii Kircheri E. Soc. Jesu. Magneticum Naturae Regnum sive Disceptatio Physiologica de triplica in Natura rerum Magnete, iuxta triplicem eiusdem Naturae gradum digesto — Inanimato, Animato, Sensitivo, qua occultae prodigiosarum quarundam motionum vires et proprietates, quae in triplici Naturae Oeconomia nonnullis in corporibus noviter delectis observavantur, in apertam lucem eruuntur et luculentis argumentis, experientia duce, demonstrantur." 1667.

This work is divided into four sections :—

Sectio I. "De viribus Naturae in genere."
Sectio II. "De Magnetibus animalis."
Sectio III. "De Magnetibus in vegetabili Natura existetibus—sive de solisequis et lunisequis Magnetibus."
Sectio IV. "De Sensitivae Naturae Magnete."

Note 2.

The following is the full title of William Maxwell's work :—

"De Medicina Magnetica Libri tres in quibus tam Theoria quam praxis continentur opus novum admirabile et utilissimum ubi multa Naturae secretissima miracula panduntur spiritus vitalis operationes hactenus incognitae revelantur, totiusque hujus secretae artis fundamenta formissimis rationibus experientia fultis porruntur: philosophiae secretioris, studiosorum gratia, Auctore Guillelmo Maxvello, M.D. Scoto-Britano." 1679.

Some of his ideas are very curious.

He seeks to prove the following twelve conclusions :—

Conclusio 1. "Anima non solum in corpore proprio visibili, sed etiam extra corpus est, nec corpore organico circumscribitur."

Conclusio 2. "Anima extra corpus proprium, communiter sic dictum, operatur."

Conclusio 3. "Ab omni corpore radii corporales fluunt, in quibus anima sua praesentia operatur; hisque energiam et potentiam operandi largitur."

Conclusio 4. "Radii hi, qui ex animalium corporibus emittuntur, spiritu vitali gaudent, per quem animae operationes dispensantur."

Conclusio 5. "Excrementa corporum animalium spiritus vitalis portionem retinent; ideoque vita illis negando non est. Estque haec vita eiusdem cum vita animalis speciei sive ab eadem anima propagatur."

Conclusio 6. "Inter corpus et excrementa a corpore procedentia, concatenatio quaedam est spiritum sive radiorum, licet excrementa longissime separentur, partium corporis separeturum, sicut et sanguinis eadem prorsus est ratio."

Conclusio 7. "Vitalitas haec tam diu durat, quam diu excrementa, sive partes separatae, vel sanguinis in aliud diversae speciei commutatus non fuerit."

Conclusio 8. "Una parte corporis affecta, sive spiritu laeso, morbida compatiuntur reliqua."

Conclusio 9. "Si spiritus vitalis in aliqua parte fortificatus fuerit, fortificatur illa ipsa actione in toto corpore."

Conclusio 10. "Ubi magis nudus est spiritus ibi citius afficitur."

Conclusio 11. "In excrementis, sanguine, etc., non tam immersus est spiritus quam in corpore, ideoque in his citius afficitur."

Conclusio 12. "Commixtio spirituum efficit compassionem a compassione illa ortum ducit."

SOME WRITINGS ON HYPNOTISM AND KINDRED SUBJECTS.

For the guidance of those who may wish to study the subject more fully, I append a list of some of the modern works. It only embraces books, and does not include any contributions to encyclopædias, reviews, etc., though in these may be found some of the best work. Many of the works below are written from entirely different standpoints, and the inclusion of any book is not necessarily an endorsement of the views maintained by its author. I shall be glad to have any omissions pointed out to me.

AZAM. *Hypnotisme, double conscience et altération de la personnalité.* Paris, 1887.
BEAUNIS. *Du Somnambulisme Provoqué.* Paris, 1886.
BELLANGER. *Le magnétisme, vérités et chimères.* Paris, 1884.
BELFIORE. *L'ipnotismo.* Naples, 1887.
BELLIDO. *Examen del hipnotismo.* Madrid, 1888.
BENTIVEGNI. *Die Hypnose und ihre civilrechtliche Bedentung.* Leipzig, 1890.
BÉRILLON. *La suggestion au point de vue pédagogique,* Paris, 1886; *Hypnotisme expérimentale,* Paris, 1884.

BERNHEIM. *De la suggestion, etc.*, Paris, 1887 (London, 1890); *Hypnotisme, Suggestion, Psycho-Thérapie* Paris, 1891.

BESSE. *De l'hypnotisme thérapeutique.* Montpellier, 1888.

BINET. *La psychologie du raisonnement, recherches expérimentales par l'hypnotisme.* Paris, 1886.

BINET ET FÉRÉ. *Le magnétisme animal.* Paris, 1887; London, 1891.

BJÖRNSTRÖM. *Hypnotismen, den utreckling och nuvärande standpunkt.* Stockholm, 1887; New York, 1890.

BOTTEY. *Le magnétisme animal.* Paris, 1884.

BOURRU ET BUROT. *Les variations de la personnalité.* Paris, 1888.

BRÜGELMANN. *Über den Hypnotismus und seine Verwertung in der Praxis.* Neuwied, 1889.

BRULLARD. *Considérations générales sur l'etat hypnotique.* Nancy, 1886.

CALATRAVEÑO. *El hypnotismo al alcance de todas las intelligencias.* Madrid, 1888.

CAMPILI. *Il grande ipnotismo e la suggestione ipnotica nei rapporti col diritto penale e civile.* Rome, 1886.

CHARCOT. *Hypnotisme, métalloscopie électrothérapie.* Paris, 1888.

COLAS. *L' hypnotisme et la volonté.* Paris, 1885.

CORY. *Hypnotism or Mesmerism.* Boston, 1888.

COSTE. *L' inconscient, etc.* Paris, 1888.

CULLERRE. *Magnétisme et hypnotisme.* Paris, 1885.

DAVID. *Magnétisme animal, suggestion hypnotique et post-hypnotique, son emploi comme agent thérapeutique.* Paris, 1887.

DELACROIX. *Les suggestions hypnotiques. Une lacune dans la loi.* Paris, 1886.

DE LAGRAVE. *Hypnotisme, états intermédiares entre le sommeil et la veille.* Paris, 1888.

DELBŒUF. *De l'Origine des Effets Curatifs de l'Hypnotisme.* Paris, 1887.

DESSOIR. *Bibliographie des Modernen hypnotismus,* Berlin, 1888; *Erster Nachtrag zur Bibliographie,* Berlin, 1890.

DICHAS. *Étude de la mémoire dans ses rapports avec le sommeil hypnotique.* Bordeaux, 1886.

DREHER. *Der Hypnotismus, seine Stellung zum Aberglauben und zur Wissenschaft.* Neuwied, 1889.

DUCLOUX. *La médecine d'imagination, les maladies imaginaires et la thérapeutique suggestive.* Montpellier, 1887.

FAJARDO. *Hipnotismo.* Rio de Janeiro, 1888.

FELKIN. *Hypnotism.* London, 1890.

FOREL. *Der Hypnotismus seine psychophyscologische medicinische.* Stuttgart, 1891.

FOREL. *Der Hypnotismus.* Stuttgart, 1889.

FONTAN ET SÉGARD. *Eléments de Médecine Suggestive.* Paris, 1887.

FRÄNKEL. *Magnetisme oz Hypnotisme.* Kjöbenhavn, 1889.

GESSMAN. *Magnetismo und Hypnotismo.* Wien, 1887.

GUERMONPREZ. *L' ipnotismo e la suggestione.* Bologna, 1888.

HERRERO. *El Hypnotismo y la Suggestion.* Valladolid, 1889.

HOEFELT. *Het hypnotisme in verband met het Strafecht.* Leiden, 1889.

HUSS. *Om hypnotismen, de vador den innebär och kan innebära.* Stockholm, 1888.

HEIDENHAIN. *Hypnotism or Animal Magnetism.* London, 1892.

JANET (PIERRE). *L'automatisme psychologique.* Paris, 1889.

KINGSBURY. *The Practice of Hypnotic Suggestion.* Bristol, 1891.

Krafft-Ebing. *Eine experimentelle Studie auf dem Gebiet des Hypnotismus.* Stuttgart, 1887; New York, 1890.

Ladame. *L'hypnotisme et la médecine légale.* Lyon, 1888.

Lafforgue. *Contribution à l'étude médico-légale de l'hypnotisme.* Bordeaux, 1887.

Liébault. *Du sommeil et des états analogues considérés au point de vue de l'action du moral sur le physique.* Paris, 1866. *Le sommeil provoqué et les états analogues.* Paris, 1889. *Thérapeutique Suggestive, son Méchanisme, etc.* Paris, 1891.

Liégois. *De la suggestion hypnotique dans ses rapports avec le droit civil et le droit criminel.* Paris, 1884. *De la suggestion et du somnambulisme dans leur rapports avec la jurisprudence et la médecine légale.* Paris, 1888.

Lutier et Havaas. *Hypnotisme et hypnotisées. La suggestion criminelle.* Paris, 1887.

Luys. *Leçons cliniques sur les principaux phénomènes de l'hypnotisme dans leur rapports avec la pathologie mentale.* Paris, 1890.

Lehmann. *Die Hypnose.* Liepsic, 1891.

Maack. *Zur Einführung in das Studium des Hypnotismus und tierischen Magnetismus.* Berlin, 1888.

Moll. *Der Hypnotismus.* Berlin, 1890; London, 1891.

Morselli. *Il magnetisme animale, la fascinazione e gli stati ipnotici.* Torino, 1886.

Myers (A. T.) *The life history of a case of double or multiplex personality.* London, 1886.

Nicoll. *Hypnotic Suggestion.* London, 1891.

Osgood. *Hypnotic Suggestion.* Boston, 1891.

Pitres. *Leçons cliniques sur l'Hysterie et l'Hypnotisme.* Paris, 1891.

Preyer. *Der Hypnotismus.* Vienna, 1890.

RAFFAELE. *La suggestione terapeutica.* Naples, 1887.
RICHER. *Etudes cliniques sur la grand hystérie ou hystéro-épilepsie.* Paris, 1885.
RICHET. *L'homme et l'intelligence.* Paris, 1884.
ROUS. *Hypnotisme et responsabilité.* Montpellier, 1887.
ROUX-FREISSINENG. *L'hypnotisme dans ses rapports avec le droit, etc.* Marseilles, 1887.
SALLIS. *Der tierische Magnetismus und seine Genese.* Leipsig, 1887. *Über hypnotische Suggestionen deren Wesen, deren Klinische und Strafrechtliche Bedentung.* Berlin, 1887.
SCHLEISNER. *Hypnotismens samfunds farlige Betydning.* Kjöbenhavn, 1888.
SCHRENCK-NOTZING. *Ein Beitrag zur therapeutischen Verwertung des Hypnotismus.* Leipsig, 1885.
SICARD. *Contribution à l'étude de l'hypnotisme et de la suggestion.* Montpellier, 1886.
TANZI. *Sulla cura suggestiva del morfinismo.* Naples, 1889.
THOMAS. *Les procès de sorcellerie et la suggestion hypnotique* Nancy, 1887.
TOURETTE. *L'hypnotisme et les états analogues au point de vue médico-légal.* Paris, 1887.
TUCKEY. *Psycho-Therapeutics.* London, 1891. *The Value of Hypnotism in Chronic Alcoholism.* London, 1892.
TUKE, HACK. *Sleep-Walking and Hypnotism.* London, 1884.
VAN EEDEN. *De psychische geneeswyse, etc.* Amsterdam, 1888.
VAN RENTERGHEM. *Hypnotisme e suggestie in de geneeskundige praktijk.* Amsterdam, 1887. *Het hypnotisme en tijne Zoepassing in de geneeskunde.* Amsterdam, 1887.

www.ingramcontent.com/pod-product-compliance
Lightning Source LLC
Chambersburg PA
CBHW022045230426
43672CB00008B/1071